A Meaningful Life

M.P. LAKHANI

BOOKS FOR ALL
DELHI-110052

Published by:
BOOKS FOR ALL
C-2/9, 3rd Floor, Community Centre,
Ashok Vihar, Phase II, Delhi-110052

Laser Typeset by:
ABC *for* DTP
6, Rajdhani Enclave, Delhi-34

Printed at:
D.K. Fine Art Press, Delhi.

Preface

What is the meaning of this life? How can we make it more meaningful? Or, why should we live?

These are the questions which have stared into our faces at one or the other time. There have also been moments when we vacillated between life and death, often under some stress caused by this or that factor. This factor may be health, it may be finance, or it may be emotional. But if one has learnt to live with equanimity, one may never experience this stress.

Equanimity is not impossible to achieve. It is possible if the laws of Nature are observed. Nature demands discipline, as it enforces discipline on itself. A disciplined life is always result-oriented. The achievers have always been a disciplined lot, may they be individuals or a nation. Japan and Germany are glaring examples.

I have tried to communicate through these pages what I acquired in the whole span of my life - ninety years. This, in a way, is quintessence of life. I want your life to be blissful. Hence this book.

M.P. Lakhani

Contents

1

Hints for Health

MASTICATION

We have to eat to live. During manual, emotional and mental work cells of the body die. New cells have to be born to take their place. During the growing age not only the dead cells need to be replaced but more are wanted for growth and development. It is food that supplies material for building new cells.

Building depends upon three factors—digestion, assimilation and elimination. If any of these three processes is faulty, health will be thrown out of gear. Proper mastication of food is an important factor for keeping these processes in good order. Every mouthful should be given about 70 bites.

A thorough mastication helps in several ways: food is swallowed easily, food is so much broken up that the digestive juices, in the digestive tract, mix intimately with it and digest it completely; it saves labour in the digestive tract for breaking up food, it promotes production and flow of saliva which is essential and particularly for the digestion of starchy food like rice and potatoes; it stimulates the heart and so the circulation of blood; it promotes health and strength of the teeth and the jaws.

Improperly masticated food entails harder labour for the digestive tract and even then it is not properly digested and is eliminated without giving strength and energy to the body, with the result that one has to eat larger quantities of food which in turn creates more labour and greater inefficiency. If food is properly masticated, body requires less quantity because it gets better digested and assimilated giving health to the body at minimum expense of quantity, labour and energy.

And a well masticated mouthful tastes so deliciously sweet! Even milk and soft foods should be churned in the mouth sufficiently long to have a good amount of saliva mixed with them.

Practise mastication yourself and teach it to your children too. It will save you a lot of bother and doctor's bill.

CARROTS

Fruit—juicy fruit - is an ideal food for man; but it does not grow in such abundance as to make it cheap enough for everybody to afford it. Nature, however, is considerate and generous and has created other things in the shape of vegetables that grow in abundance and are, thus, within the reach of almost all. Carrot is one such item. Carrot is one of the best eatables that Nature has given to Man.

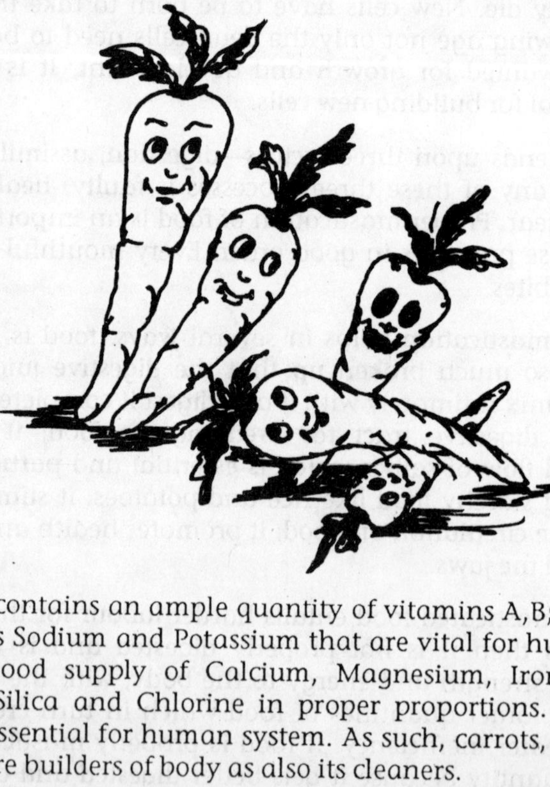

Carrot contains an ample quantity of vitamins A,B,C,D,E,G and K; it contains Sodium and Potassium that are vital for human health; it gives a good supply of Calcium, Magnesium, Iron, Phosphorus, Sulphur, Silica and Chlorine in proper proportions. These organic salts are essential for human system. As such, carrots, if taken raw or as juice, are builders of body as also its cleaners.

By virtue of their vitamin and salt contents, carrots increase appetite and help digestion; nourish and protect the nervous system; improve and maintain bone structure of teeth; enrich mother's milk; help prevent infection of eyes, throat, tonsils, sinuses and respiratory organs; correct dry skin, dermatitis and other skin blemishes; give strength to eyes and the optical system; increase vigour and vitality; help correct liver and intestinal disorders; invigorate endocrine glands; are of great help during pregnancy. Carrots, thus, if taken in sufficient quantity will nourish and maintain the health of the intestinal, nervous and respiratory systems. They will adjust the chemical balance of the body and adjust its weight.

Cooking of carrots decreases their vitamin efficiency but still they are a useful item of diet. A dishful of carrot salads will be a wonderful help and it is so cheap.

SKIN AND BATH

Blood circulates through the blood vessels of the skin and gets heated or cooled according to the temperature of the surroundings. In cold weather, the blood vessels of the skin contract and so prevent much of our blood from circulation. This preserves the body heat. In hot weather, the blood vessels dilate and excrete perspiration which while evaporating cools the circulating blood and so the body. Within reasonable limits, the skin adjusts itself and one can stand coldness and heat without feeling discomfort. But if the skin becomes sluggish and loses its capacity to adjust to the changing temperature of the surroundings, cold and heat become distressing. It is, therefore, necessary to keep the skin in fit condition.

Bath regulates the heat of the body. In hot weather cold bath extracts heat from the body and in cold weather, warm water conveys heat to the body. Cold water causes the blood vessels to contract with the result the blood is drawn inwards, away from the surface of the skin. This is followed by a reaction so that the blood comes back with a rush causing warmth and glow. On the other hand, hot water dilates the blood vessels with the result that the blood is pushed outwards to the skin causing comfort and warmth. Effect in both the cases is a more rapid and gushing surface circulation of blood. This breaks down local congestion and blood reaches larger areas and with increased force, producing greater oxidation and pushing unwanted matter more quickly to the organs of elimination. It also stimulates the activity of the tissue cells and has a pronounced beneficial effect on the nervous system, thus increasing the nerve-force. The ebb and flow of blood is an important factor for the health of the skin and should be encouraged by pouring colder water over the body after a warm bath. Care should be taken not to chill the body. The temperature of cold water should be so adjusted that after the cold water pouring, the body must feel a glow of warmth.

Only hot baths accustom the skin to function at higher temperatures, with the result that the person becomes susceptible to cold. The hotter the water one uses, more susceptible to cold he becomes.

RELAXATION

Nervous diseases and nervousness are on the increase. In the present day civilisation of hurry and worry, the nervous strain is great without any compensating relief to the nervous system. The result is that the nervous system becomes weaker and weaker and gets out of control.

The symptoms of nervousness are naturally more visible among the city-dwellers, because noise, speed and worry assail them incessantly. When you find anybody fidgetty, tapping his foot while sitting or shaking his leg, cracking knuckles, twitching involuntarily any part of his body, wrinkling his forehead, tearful, depressed, jittery, well, he is suffering from nervous strain. He is urgently in need of relaxation—physical and mental. Neglect of the symptoms may well lead to neurasthenia or nervous breakdown.

He is apt to work with taut nerves at high pressure, thereby exhausting himself. Heavy work can be done with relaxed mind and body at much less expense of nervous energy. All great workers follow this method. Annie Besant, Gandhiji and others worked for eighteen to twenty hours a day and yet were much less tired than an ordinary person working for only five to six hours a day. What is necessary is the correct reaction to one's work and the knack of closing one's mind to disturbing and irritating external stimuli.

Mind has tremendous effect on the body. It needs diversion, at regular intervals, from the usual work, into play and recreation.

To remove tension from muscles and nerves and to gain energy by relaxation, control of mind and body is essential. Sit or lie down in a comfortable posture with eyes closed and consciously relax each part of the body from top downwards; nape of the neck, face, shoulders, arms, back, chest, abdomen, upper legs, lower legs and feet. And then make the mind blank. Blankness of mind is not sleep; it is a sweet calm state of being without thoughts; a state of vague consciousness. The sign of proper relaxation is that you will be unconscious of your body. You will not know in what position your arm or foot is lying. Try to become conscious of your arm or leg, you cannot; you will have to put forth effort to lift your arm or leg before you can become conscious of it. A few minutes of this repose produces the same beneficial effect as a few hours of sleep.

A relaxed mind and body during work means less fatigue and more efficient work. It is worth trying. Practise relaxation few times a day. In course of time, you will find that it has become a habit.

MASSAGE

Our body consists of muscles, tissues, nerves etc. All these are made up of cells. Cell is the final unit. Body, thus is a colony of millions of cells. Every cell does its own special work. Every piece of work, whether mechanical, emotional or mental is done by these cell-workers and while doing their work, they get exhausted and die and their place is taken by new cells that are being born. At every moment of our existence, some cells are dying and others are being born to replace them.

The dead cells are waste matter and should be eliminated. This is achieved by the circulating blood which carries it to the excretory organs which throw it out of the body. In addition, the circulating blood supplies the ingredients for the formation of new cells giving life and vigour to the body. The better the circulation of blood, the more efficient will be the elimination and building. Bad circulation will mean clogging up of the blood channels with dead matter, which will make the health deteriorate. Poor circulation of blood should, therefore, receive external help in just the same way as a blocked up gutter or nali requires vigorous flushing to make the waste matter move on.

After walking, working or doing any manual work as also after mental work or nervous strain, one feels tired. This feeling of fatigue is due to the dead cell matter clogging up the blood channels. The cells die more quickly than they can be removed. Rest removes fatigue because blood in course of time, removes waste matter.

When we feels uncomfortably tired, shampooing or massage give quick relief. Massage is an external help to increase the circulation of blood with the result that it exerts greater force and removes the waste matter quickly. Atheletes go in for massage immediately after the exercise. Racing horses are given a massage immediately after they have run in the race. Massage removes physical, mental and nervous fatigue; it relaxes and refreshes the body and mind.

Massage once or twice a week will go a long way in keeping the body in good health.

2
Sleep

Sleep in supposed to refresh and invigorate. But increasingly more people have started complaining that they wake up from sleep tired. Many complain of sleeplessness and have recourse to sleeping pills.

Man must sleep. Everybody sleeps : men, animals, birds, vegetation. We must also get the best out of sleep. There is a wrong way of sleeping and there is a right way of sleeping. Everyone would like to sleep the right way to get the maximum out of it.

During the day, one is active, engaged in various activities wherein every organ of the body participates and emotional and mental faculties are exercised. Some organs of the body are exercised voluntarily — like arms, legs, eyes, etc., while other organs like digestive system, lungs, heart etc., act involuntarily, without one's conscious effort. Organs get fatigued and need rest to recoup, to get 're-charged' for more work, and this is achieved during sleep.

It is a common experience that when one is physically and mentally tired, a short nap—forty winks—refreshes and makes one ready to resume work. It seems there is some cosmic energy that enters one's organism during sleep, repairs the wear and tear and leaves one fresh.

Several factors affect sleep: the direction in which one lies, temperature, light, ventilation, noise, time, qualitative and quantitative contents of the stomach, position of the body, mental state etc.

Our ancients knew the effect these factors produced; they have left behind advice based on scientific principles, in accordance with the laws of Nature.

For example, Garga Rishi has said that man should lie down with his head towards east. But if he wants longevity, he should lie down with his head south-ward. And if he is not in his house but elsewhere, he may have his head west-ward. But nowhere should he lie down with his head towards north.

Sage Markandya has said that while sleeping, one should lie down with one's head east-ward. This makes one intelligent. By having one's head south-ward, one gains strength and longevity. But one invites disease and death if one sleeps with one's head north-ward.

Vishnu Puran says that it is helpful to lie down with one's head east-ward or south-ward. But he who lies in other directions will attract ill-health.

Why?

It is a common knowledge that earth is a huge magnet with its geographic north pole as magnetic north pole and its geographic south pole as magnetic south pole. Also north pole of one magnet repels north pole of another magnet but attracts its south pole; and south pole repels the south pole of another magnet and attracts its north pole.

Earth has also an electric current going round it from east to west, with east as positive electrode and west as negative electrode. This current is produced by the heat of the sun. Since sun rises in the east, the east side of the earth becomes warm by the rising sun while the west side remains cold. This difference of temperature between the two sides produces a thermal electric current traversing the surface of the earth from east to west.

Attention also needs to be drawn to one more scientific fact: where an electric current enters, i.e., at the positive electrode (anode) coldness is produced and where the current leaves the body, i.e. at the negative electrode (Cathode), heat is produced.

Medical science tells us that the human body is capable of being magnetised and it is also an electric conductor. There are magnetic and electric circuits in the human body.

Man has his feet on earth. In the northern hemisphere, the earth has north magnetic polarity and hence, in accordance with the laws of science, south polarity is induced at the feet and north polarity at head. Thus man becomes a magnet with his feet as south pole and his head as north pole. Man's health and well-being is conditioned to be the best with this arrangement. If this arrangement is disturbed, it will produce disturbance in his body, resulting in disease and ill-health.

When a person sleeps with his head in the south and feet in the north, the earth's magnetic north pole attracts his magnetic south pole (feet) and earth's magnetic south pole attracts his magnetic north pole (head), and thus preserves the magnetic field of his body. This induces good, refreshing sleep and allows the sleep to produce its beneficial effect. If, however, he sleeps with his head towards the north and feet towards the south, there will be repulsion at both the ends, which will disturb the magnetic field of his body and will result in disturbed sleep and ill-health.

If a man sleeps with his head towards the east, the electric current, going from east to west over the surface of the earth, will pass through him, entering at the head and going out at the feet. Since the current, at its point of entrance produces coldness, it will remove heat and congestion from his brain, making it healthy and more efficient and will make his feet warmer as it leaves his body. If he were to sleep with his head towards the west, the current, entering at the feet will make them cooler and make the head warmer and congested. This condition is contrary to the health of the body. It is a well-known medical dictum that for good health, one should keep one's feet warm, stomach soft (good elimination) and head cool.

Sleep is induced easily in a cool place rather than in a warm place. How cool a place needs to be depends upon each individual. In a particular season, one person may sleep with a covering, while another without a covering, and yet another with fan working full blast.

One sleeps better in a darkened room than in a room with a light on.

Sleep in a well-ventilated room is not so sound as in a less ventilated room. This is because less oxygen in the blood in conducive to better sleep. Animals sleep with their paws across the nose to decrease the intake of air, and thereby lessen the quantity of oxygen inhaled. Birds tuck their beaks under their wings. Persons who sleep all wrapped up—head and face—sleep more soundly.

How does noise affect sleep? A monotonous sound, howsoever strong, (ticking of a clock, regular noise of an engine) induces sleep, but a sudden unexpected sound, even opening of a door or a foot step, may wakeup a sleeper.

Time/ factor is not of a less importance. Medical opinion says that sleep before midnight is more beneficial and restful than that after midnight. "Early to bed and early to rise makes one healthy, wealthy and wise."

A heavy stomach causes disturbed sleep. To digest a heavy meal, stomach has to do extra work. It is therefore, essential to go to bed not less than one hour after the night meal. A late heavy meal should be avoided.

People adopt all sorts of positions during sleep. In fact, some postures are grotesque. Body should be trained to adopt a correct and graceful posture during sleep. Curling up into a C- shape, like a cat, curves the spine and is likely to cause stooping. Sleeping on the back allows the tongue to fall backwards, obstructing breathing and producing snoring. Generally, one does not snore while lying on a side. Sleeping on the back is likely to give hump-shoulders. Sleeping on sides will strain neck muscles on one side and cramp them on the other. This may ultimates affect one's carriage and poise. Too high a pillow causes various discomforts. The best posture to adopt is to have a pillow just high enough to keep the head in line with the spine and to lie down on a side with legs outstretched, so that the head, the spine and the legs are more or less in a straight line. The arms should be along the side or bent. This position is not only graceful but prevent cramping of any organ and does not hinder it from doing it normal work. Posture is a matter of habit. Habit of correct posture can be cultivated.

Sleep is a necessity. Not only that, sufficient sleep is a necessity. A normal human being needs eight hours of sleep. A mental worker needs more sleep than a physical worker. Less sleep, in course of time, produces ever-increasing fatigue, inefficiency and irritability. The process may be slow - it generally is - and one may not be conscious of the progressive damage being done to one's physical and mental health.

Good, refreshing sleep, specially an after-lunch nap, keeps the complexion smooth, soft and unwrinkled.

When one goes to bed unrelaxed and worried the brain keeps working, the emotions affecting the facial expression. This produces the habit of contortion of face.

To be able to have a sound and beneficial sleep, one needs to be physically and mentally relaxed, and without worry and anxiety and over-wrought nerves. Excitement prevents sleep.

Sleeplessness is the result of over-working of the brain. When thoughts, worries and emotions keep crowding in, sleep stays out. In such a case, a deliberate effort to relax mind and muscle will help a great deal. Activity of the brain can be arrested by reducing the blood going into it. This may be achieved by binding tightly a kerchief or a piece of cloth round the forehead; or even by keeping an arm on the forehead. A cup of warm milk or ovaltine at the time of going to bed will soothe the nerves.

Relaxation is an art which everyone must practise and master. Relaxation not only helps in getting good sleep, but also prevents unnecessary wear and tear of the body and mind and this preserves energy and maintains physical and mental poise.

The technique of relaxation is quite easy. Sit down comfortably, in an easy chair, or lie down. Starting with the neck muscles, direct the muscles to relax. After the neck muscles, instruct the muscles of the shoulders, arms, back, waist, chest, stomach, pelvis, thighs, lower legs and feet to do the same. The test of relaxation is that the relaxed parts become heavy as dead parts. If your eyes are closed and you want to know where your foot or leg or hand is, you will not know. If you try to move it, it will feel heavy and you will have to exert in order to move it. If your eyes are open, you are seeing where, your hand is, but to move it you will have to employ force more than you normally do. You will be surprised at the phenomenon. Thus, after you have relaxed the body, direct your mind to become blank. Thoughts will come crowding in. Don't get annoyed; give them appointments for the next day and firmly refuse to entertain them 'immediates'. A little practice will make you achieve the result. When body and mind get relaxed, sleep walks in. If, during the day, you want to refresh yourself, relax while sitting in an easy chair or in an easy posture - in a few minutes you will feel fine.

Periods of deep sleep and light sleep alternate during the sleep. All sleep at night is not all deep or all light. Starting with deep sleep, lasting for about an hour, it starts becoming light till around 3 a.m. it is lightest and one may even wake up momentarily and then doze off into deep sleep like the first one. This again becomes light around 6-7 a.m. when most people getup. But if instead of getting up at this time when sleep is lightest, one permits one's self a doze-off which is the beginning of another period of deep sleep and then wake up after a short while to be in time for work, one feels un-refreshed and weak. Hence it is best to get out of bed at the time of light sleep.

Everybody dreams. Some remember their dreams, other do not, and say that they do not have dreams. During the periods of deep sleep, duration of dreams is short, from 6 to 8 minutes. As the sleep becomes lighter, the duration of dreams increases, going up to 20-24 minutes.

Nature has its own way of working. During youth and middle age, one may defy laws of Nature and seem to get away with it. But Nature never forgives and one has to pay heavily for the defiance in later life, when resistance is less, when every organ of the body is weak. Then all sorts of ailments attack the body and the mind and suffering becomes great.

To sum up:

1. One should sleep with head towards south. Second best, towards east. Never towards north. This is true in the Northern hemisphere; it'll just be opposite in the Southern hemisphere.

2. Sleep in a cool place.
3. Sleep in a darkened room.
4. Sleep early, before midnight.
5. Sleeping room should not be highly ventilated.
6. Do not go to bed with a heavy stomach.
7. Do not use a high pillow.
8. Cultivate a proper posture while sleeping.
9. Be physically and mentally relaxed while going to bed.
10. Sleep for sufficient time, on an average for 8 hours.
11. Get up during lighter period of sleep.

3
Honey

From time immemorial, honey has been used as food. It is considered as Nature's most perfect and easily assimilable food. Sugar, before it can be digested, is broken up into grape sugar and other assimilable sugars. This means extra work for stomach. Honey has ready grape-sugar which is immediately assimilated, giving instantaneous energy. All ingredients of honey are assimilable. Honey and ripe sweet fruits are finest energy producers, containing purest form of sugars.

Honey is a mixture of sugars obtained from flowers by the honey-bee. Honey-bee, attracted by the colour and fragrance of flowers sucks nectar from them. The nectar is a watery fluid of flavour peculiar to the flower from which it is taken. Honey is not monofloral but multi-floral, i.e. the nectar is not collected from one type of flower, but from a number of different flowers. Bees take nectar from more than 10,000 kinds of flowers. Mono-floral honey could be had only if an apiary is confined to an area where only one type of flowers are grown. A honey, though multi-floral, is usually named after the flower whose flavour is the most dominant. Nectar collected by the bees is deposited in the honey-comb where it undergoes transformation, loses water and becomes thick and sweeter. By the time, honey is ready in the honey-comb, nectar has been reduced to one-third of its original quantity. The nectar collected from each flower is so little that it takes 10,000 collections to make one teaspoonful of honey. Colour of the honey depends upon the flowers from which nectar is collected. The colour could be light, dark, creamy white, amber, brown, purple, ruby, greenish, and black.

Stomach is not conditioned to absorb sugar. Sugar when taken is converted by the enzymes—Invertase and Amylase—in the stomach to dextrose and levulose sugars which are absorbed when they reach intestines. Honey is a pre-digested sugar, the greater part being dextrose and levulose. When these sugars reach small intestines, they are absorbed and get into the blood stream. While dextrose is immediately absorbed and converted into energy, levulose is carried to the liver where it is converted to glycogen and stored there to be released when body requires it. When so released, glycogen is converted into dextrose and used. Honey is the richest source of levulose and is twice as sweet as cane sugar. In the body, sugars are converted into heat and energy. That is why body demands more sugar in cold climate and cold seasons and after physical exertion. If levulose is taken more than can be stored by the liver, the excess gets transformed into fat.

Honey contains various ingredients : Sugar, principally dextrose and levulose and varying quantities of sucrose, dextrine, maltose and some other rare sugars. Mineral contents of honey are: iron, copper, manganese, magnesium, calcium, potassium, silica, chlorine and phosphorus. The darker the honey, the greater the amount of iron, copper and manganese in it. The acid contents are : formic, acetic, malic, citric, succinic and amino-acids. It also contains pigments carotin and xanthophyll, albuminoids, traces of volatile acids and digested fats. It contains enzymes invertase, diastase, catalase and invulase. Vitamin contents are: riboflavin 0.26 (B), nicotinic acid 1.1 (B), thiamine 0.044(B1), pyridoxin 0.10 (B6), biotin 0.00066 (B) and folic acid 0.03 (B). There will be some variation in the contents of honey from different sources, depending upon the soil on which the flowers grow, but every sample, more or less, contains the same proportion of dextrose and levulose.

In these days of adulteration, it is necessary to test the purity of honey. The best test, perhaps, is that when it is allowed to flow out in a very thin stream on to a surface, it will fall on the surface in snake-like coils. Adulterated honey will run smoothly like any other fluid without making snaky coils.

Because of its varied constituents, apart from it being Nature's perfect food, it is used for a variety of purposes :

Micro-organisms of various disease can thrive only when they have some amount of moisture. If the moisture is withdrawn from them, they die. Potassium (contained in the honey) has the property of absorbing moisture. Honey contains potassium; hence honey absorbs moisture from bacteria in contact with honey and they soon perish. So honey is used as a disinfectant. When applied to skin burns or scalds, it relieves pain and smarting, prevents formation of blisters, heals rapidly, leaving no scars behind. It prevents wounds from becoming gangrenous. Honey, mixed with cod-liver oil, is useful in festering wounds. It is used in cuts. When applied to bleeding cuts, it arrests bleeding and heals the cut quickly without leaving a scar.

Honey is a good preservative. Honey itself needs no preservatives; it can keep good indefinitely.

Its iron content makes it useful in anemia. Iron carries oxygen to the body tissues and increases the hemoglobin of the blood. Copper and manganese help iron in this function. It normalises blood composition.

In gastro-intestinal disturbances, iron and magnesium help digestion. Hence honey is useful in digestive troubles. It decreases acidity. It prevents fomentation in the stomach. Honey sugar does not irritate the digestive tract and it does not tax the kidneys. It acts as a gentle laxative.

Honey is a quick restorative for fatigued atheletes. Sugar, in the body, is converted into heat and energy. Since honey sugar is pre-digested and easily assimilated, it is an immediate source of energy, and removes fatigue after physical exertion.

Cramps in muscles, particularly in legs and soles or feet, occurring at night, are relieved in a week's time by taking two teaspoonfuls of honey at each meal. Twitching of eye-lids and corners of mouth are likewise controlled by taking honey as in the case of cramps.

Liver acts as a filter, keeping bacterial toxins from entering the blood. Glycogen helps in this process and thereby increases the body's resistance to infection. That is why glucose is given to patients intravenously.

Honey is excellent for heart ailments. About 70 gms. of honey daily for about two months produces marked improvement. It also soothes the nerves of the nervous people. High strung people benefit from it. It is good for insomnia. A tablespoonful of honey with night meal will go a long way to help. It may be mixed with the juice of a lemon in a cupful of warm water and taken before retiring. Licking honey or a mixture of honey and juice of lemon give relief in cough.

Honey builds sturdy bones and teeth when fed to infants. Infants fed on honey will not suffer from colic because honey sugar is absorbed quickly and fermentation does not take place. If a mother cannot nurse her child on her milk and other milk has to be given, addition of honey to the milk will provide almost all the ingredients required for the baby. Child fed with honey will rarely suffer from vomiting or diarrhoea.

Bed-wetting is not uncommon in children. Such chiidren are generally of a nervous type. Among other things, a teaspoonful of honey at bed-time would be useful. Honey will soothe the nerves, act as a sedative and bring on good sleep. It will absorb and hold the fluid in the child's body till morning.

Pure, clarified honey, specially lotus honey or neem honey could be used as 'kajal' and will benefit. It could be used for cataract, inflamation, aching, burning and tired feeling etc.

Honey is heat giving. But it can provide a very cooling and nourishing drink in summer. Take a tablespoonful of honey or quantity of taste in a glass of water. Take another empty glass and pour the contents in it. Repour the contents into the first glass and so on, for over 50 times. In so doing, the honeyed water takes up 'prana' or cosmic energy from the atmosphere. It also becomes a delicious, cooling sherbet, more cooling than other sherbets. It is also excellent for any summer stomach derangement.

Honey could be used by diabetics without any harm. Because of its various ingredients and properties, it is also used in ointments and medicines, whether allopathic, ayurvedic, unani or homoeopathic.

4

Breasts—Woman's Charm : Its Care and Culture

If woman had no breasts, would she command a second look or constitute such an attraction as she does now? Man being what he is, I believe not. Both sexes have their regions of attraction, regions that scream for attention. Breasts are one such region.

Nature is wonderful in her economy. She makes several points with one stroke. Breasts give woman beauty of form. They switch on desire to entrap two bodies into carrying on the task of procreation and help make the process easier. They provide sustenance to the new-comer help to bring the body, distended from child-birth, back to its normal proportions.

Such an important part of a woman's body needs attention and care to keep it in proper condition so that it can fulfil its functions efficiently and usefully.

It is not necessary to point out that right curves at right places and satisfactory vital statistics are an asset to a woman. Breasts find a prominent place in that scheme. They vary in size and shape as much as noses, mouths or faces do. There is an infinite variety of them, though they can be confined to a few types. What shape and what size should one have? Just that which goes harmoniously with the rest of the body, that which suits one's personality.

Breasts and liver are two very useful and tough parts of the human body. They do not go out of order easily, but once they do so, it is not easy to get them back to normal. It is, therefore, all the more necessary to pay attention to the culture and care of breasts from childhood.

In unmarried girls, the breasts should be firm, elastic, hemispherical, with small, undeveloped nipples, surrounded by deep brown areolae in brown coloured ones and pink in fair coloured ones. They become large and flabby by frequent handling and excessive marital exercise. During pregnancy, they become full, increase in size and feel tender; the nipples develop, become harder, firmer and more prominent; the areolae become darker and wider.

Breast is an easy target for cancer. As soon as any lump or hardness develops, even though it be painless, it is wise to consult a doctor immediately. Quite often, unmarried girls get hard lumps in the breasts. These, often, are not fore-runners of cancer, but are caused by frequent excitement and unsatisfied desire and can be cured easily.

A shapely, firm bosom lends beauty and dignity to the body. It also commands social advantage; while a flabby, drooping bosom gives inferiority complex, even though the present external aids simulate firmness.

How can one acquire a good bust?

The breast contains no muscle. It contains only soft tissue and fibrous strings. The fibrous strings give breast its form, position and firmness. If the strings are over-strained, the breasts lose shape and firmness. They sag and become pendulous.

Then there is the pectoral muscle. It is a muscle that runs from shoulder to shoulder, across the body, above the bust. Breasts lie on the surface of this muscle and cover it. A well-developed, filled-out pectoral muscle pushes the breasts upwards. At its upper surface, it is in contact with the mammary gland. The mammary gland itself is small and cannot be developed by exercise. But it is embedded in abundance of fat, and the quantity of fat can be increased to fill out the breasts.

Intercostal muscles of the ribs, lying beneath the breasts, offer an important support to the bust. Any exercise that will strengthen these muscles will help improve the figure.

Thus, in order to get a properly sized, shapely and firm bosom, one has to have well-developed pectoral and intercostal muscles, and tight, elastic fibrous strings. Then one can keep up one's figure even after child-birth. The muscles can be developed by exercise, while fat can be increased by oil massage. Dry, undernourished skin of the bust gives withered, sagging breasts. Deep breathing and any exercise that develops the pectoral and the intercostal muscles will help. But perhaps the best exercise is 'skipping', about thirty times, morning and evening. Any pulling exercise like rowing, pushing a pram, working a lawn mower, singing, deep breathing, are also useful.

If skipping is not practicable, try this one for the pectoral muscle. Take a deep breath, extend arms in front, palms of the two hands touching. Move the arms outwards, taking them as far back as possible. Then bring them back to the first position and while doing so, exhale slowly. Repeat the exercise five times.

For intercostal muscles: Lie down on the floor with arms by the sides of the body. Inhale slowly and at the same time raise the arms over the head. Take them further back wards and attempt to touch the floor with your hands. Then, exhaling slowly, bring the arms to the original position. Repeat the exercise five times.

Deep breathing helps improve the bust. Take slowly a full, deep breath, pushing the abdomen and the chest out. While exhaling, the chest and the abdomen move in. Starting with five, gradually increase at the rate of three per week to twenty. Breathe twice daily.

To stimulate the oils under the skin and to nourish the fat contents of the breasts as also to further increase the fat content, massage the breasts with warm olive oil. Night is the best time for breast massage. While massaging, the stroking should be in upward and outward direction—never downward.

Dragging the breasts downwards should always be avoided. Stooping over a desk or a table, half reclining in an easy chair, any habitual posture that involves forward bending, will, in course of time, make the breast tissues lose their elasticity and produce sagging. Sizeable breasts should have light support even in bed to keep them from being dragged.

Anything that helps lift the breasts would improve the figure. Sitting and standing postures which keep the spine vertical are worth cultivating. Leaning backwards helps uplift.

If the breasts are too small, they can be developed by exercise, deep breasting and ten to fifteen minute massage. In addition, hot and cold bathing of the breasts, morning and night, would be of great help. Bathe the chest with warm water for a few minutes, massage with a few drops of olive oil, then bathe or sponge it with cold water for a few minutes.

Recent engagement, marriage or any other excitement that causes glandular disturbance, may cause reduction in the size of breasts. But this effect is temporary, and as soon as the glandular activity is re-established, the previous size would be regained.

Decreasing the size of over-developed breasts poses a problem. The size can be reduced only by eliminating fat from them: and this means the same thing as slimming. Unless slimming is carried out under expert guidance, reduced breasts will become saggy and pendulous.

If due to illness or any other reason, the breasts have withered and sag, it is possible to put them in shape with patience and perseverences. Take a fifteen minutes warm olive-oil massage every night, using as much oil as can get absorbed. Beginning from the base of the breasts, let the massaging strokes be outward and upward towards the shoulders. During the massage, support the breast with on hand. When ones, put a cotton wool pad under the breasts, and bandage them so that they are raised high up on the chest. Complete the process by a ten-minute exercise to stimulate the muscles. Try dry swimming.

It is necessary to guide girls in adolescence whose bust development is rapid. If they use tight, restricting bandages, breast tissues will be cramped and get flattened. Also, the breast fibres will lose their elasticity and the possessor will be left with drooping, saggy breasts.

For the same reason, use the wrong type of brassiere is likely to produce the same defect and it may also happen that continued pressure at wrong places might permanently swell and enlarge the mammary glands. Brassiere should be such that not only it does not flatten the breasts, but it supports and uplifts them. Over-developed breasts require all the greater care in choosing proper type of brassiere for them.

Even when breasts are of proper size, shape and firmness, they, more than any other part of the body, require constant care. It is necessary that after the morning bath they are given a five-minute bath with ice-cold water in summer and cold water in winter, followed by a gentle massage with diluted eau-de-cologne, methylated spirit or whisky.

While feeding a child, the mother should sit up so that the child may not have to pull at the breast and spoil its shape. This will also avoid unnecessary strain on the neck of the child. If the supply of milk is inadequate for the child pulls harder at the nipples and for a long time, and this often cracks the nipples.

5
Kiss : Its Origin and Evolution

Kiss is a caress given with lips. Lips and tongue are littered with nerve endings so that caress with them produces pleasure.

Birds procure food and keep it in their beaks and introduce it into the mouths of their young ones. In the pre-historic days, in the days of cave-dwellers, there was no vessel for drinking water. The water was either lapped up or sucked up. The mother filled her mouth with water and transferred it to the mouth of the infant to assuage its thirst. In so doing, she kissed the lips and the mouth of the young one, and also while transferring the food from her mouth to that of the infant, she adjusted the temperature of the food to suit the delicacy of the babe's oral mucous membrane. She thus discovered the thrill of the touch and would convey it to her mate by pressing her lips on to his. To the male also, the thrill was a revelation. This is probably how the kiss was discovered. First, it was a maternal kiss.

The word 'kiss' is derived from the Latin 'gustus', signifying 'taste'. Hence, the expression 'I want to taste your face'. The kiss among ancient and uncivilised people was unknown as a symbol and harbinger of love, and it sprang from entirely the maternal act of feeding the young ones, as is practised by birds, and very often by savages.

Animals and birds also kiss.

In the pre-Christian era, lip kiss was not prevalent. In Greek mythology, kiss does not occur while the love scenes between Venus and Mars. Ulysses and Circe, Paris and Helen or Hera and Zeus are described. In the scene with Andromache, Hector, while advising her does not kiss her but caresses her hand. In ancient Egypt, kiss meant embrace and not the kissing with lips.

Homer describes how the servants of Odysses kissed his head, shoulders and hands. He also states which class of servants was entitled to pay homage in this manner and which class had to be satisfied with a hand shake. In Rome, it was customary to kiss the head, the hands, or the feet of the prominent men, according to the rank of those who saluted.

Among the Jews, however, kiss was quite common. Even mere acquaintances kissed each others' hand, head and shoulder while they exchanged the salutation, "Peace be with you". If they desired to express their highest esteem for somebody, they kissed his feet and even his footprints. Judas kissed the Messiah because this mode of salutation was a common practice. Jesus, however, did not look upon the kiss as a mere formality but as a token of love. He, therefore, asked Judas 'Do you betray the son of Man with a kiss?' and hence the Judas' kiss has become a token of treachery.

This type of kiss was borrowed by the Christians from the Jews. The first Christians knew only brotherly and sisterly kiss. Later it became customary that all members of a congregation, prior to the communion service, would exchange the 'osculum pacis', the kiss of peace. For this purpose, there were tablets introduced which passed from hand to hand. In the Greek Catholic Church, the so-called Easter kiss is still customary. People of the same faith kiss each other when they meet at Easter with the salutation. 'The Lord is risen' to which the response is made 'The Lord is risen, indeed!'.

The Roman Catholic Church introduced the kiss as a symbol of veneration for the Pope by kissing the cross embroidered on the top of the Papal slipper. In the case of Bishops, the ring worn on the right index finger is kissed. At present, visitors greeting the Pope kiss his ring on bended knees.

In Roman times, kiss was a formal symbol of goodwill, but later on, it became too promiscuous amounting to nuisance. During the reign of Ramulus, males kissed females to find out whether they had partaken of wine, which was prohibited to the women.

Greeks had a law providing that any man who kissed a woman in public should suffer death.

The Cencon Cato promulgated a law prohibiting married people from kissing each other in the presence of their children.

In ancient Rome, law provided that if a married woman permitted anybody to kiss her, she lost her dower. On the other hand, if a betrothed was kissed by her dying affianced in the presence of a third person, she was declared to be the lawful wife, and after his death, she was entitled to receive half of his estate. There are several countries where, at the present time, the kiss of betrothal has a legal effect.

During the evolution of kiss, in medievel times, it acquired different significance. The Vassal was compelled to kiss the sword of his feudal lord. In courts, the crucifix or the Bible is kissed as a symbol of truthfulness.

In Austria, it is considered good breeding to kiss the hand of women. In Spain, males must be satisfied with the verbel 'kiss your hand'. In Italy, the hand-kissing of a woman is a sign of great intimacy. In the USSR, forehead is kissed. The Russians present salutes his lord by embracing his knees and kissing them. The Pole kisses the shoulder of his superior and the Czech kisses his clothes.

Among the Druids, kiss under the Mistletoe was considered a kiss of peace.

Kissing the hand of the Royalty is a mark of feality. Kissing one's hem of skirt is an act of homage. Kissing the hand of a benefactor is the kiss of gratitude. Thus, kisses can be of many types meaning many things.

Kiss evolving through several states has now reached the stage where it is an expression of love and passion. Kiss is defined as a pressure with the lips, long or brief, silent or noisy, which, when the object kissed is the mouth of one of the opposite sex, produces a delicious exhilaration.

The thrill resulting from the pressing lips together is the mingling of soul current resulting from placing in close contact the extremities of the two sets of labial nerves. It is something like two electric wires coming together. When the positive and the negative are a little distance apart, there is sound and sparks between the two ends of the wires—a beautiful phenomenon. When the wires are placed in contact, the electricity passes without sound and sparking—the emotion is exhausted.

In the East, in India, kiss was known earlier. In ancient Sanskrit poetry, the kiss is always maternal and the 'kussiani' (Sanskrit for kiss) is exclusively filial, although later books go so far as to differentiate twelve varieties of the kiss. The wife of Califo, in Ramayana, bewailing his death, recalls the hand, not the lips that caressed her. Vatsayana, in his Kama Sutra says: Kiss should be imprinted on the loved one on forehead, eyes, cheeks, chest, breasts, lips, interior of mouth to excite the partner to the finale.

Who kissed first—man or woman? The question has been answered by an understanding and imaginative writer, thus:

In the beginning, Adam lived alone on earth without a mate. He saw nature around him; birds and animals playing and companioning each other. He felt lonely and useless. One morning, on waking, he found sleeping by his side his exact counterpart, his second self, but yet his opposite - Eve. She then woke, wound her arms about his neck and drew him upon her breast and said: "I am thy lover, wife, helpmate. Without me, you can never know why all these objects round about thee, and which thou hast so oft surveyed have been created. Long hast thou wondered, and within thy breast hast asked why thou wert apart from all the rest, the only one that missed perfection's boon. Nay, go not thou away. Thou must fulfil what fate has had in store for thee. Thou art all my ardent fancy pictured thee, and for thee, by my own strong desire, did I become incarnate that my soul with thine might round out a full existence. Thy life was vacuous and stale, and though the highest and the best of all created things, yet were thou the most useless of them all. Thou hast a troubled look and dost not comprehend. Well, then, I will convey to thee what knowledge I possess. But thou must listen and must not try to leave me. We are to be the founders of a mighty race. From us will spring a myriad hosts to circle all the earth, and through the peopling of the twinkling star thou seest above thee in the blue empyrean, a race whose future joys are concentrated within my breast, and in my soul I feel the choice delights of future ages of our kind, for in me are the energy and essence of them all. I am the fruit which thou must pluck and eat, and then thine eyes shall opened be and like unto the gods we shall become. Thou art the active, I the passive one. It is for thee to act, for me to yield."

Kisses have been described as:

> ardent, affectionate, burning, balmy, cold, divine, deep-drawn, dewy, eager, frozen, frigid, fragrant, forced, flaming, false, gentle, hallowed, impassioned, impressive, lingering, nervous, poisonous, ravishing, rapturous, smacking, soothing, soft, sacred, timid, tender, tempting, unwilling, warm.

Kiss during its evolution through the ages has acquired different meanings and corresponding epithets—

> The balm of love, Cupid's seal, The Lover's Fee, The Fee of parting, Homage of the lips, Hostage of promise, Lover's language, Love's mintage, Love's print, Love's tribute, Love's rhetoric, Nectar of Venus, Path to heaven and hell, stamp of love, Pledge of bliss and love, Seal of bliss, Melting sip, Nectar of life.

Herrick defines kiss as 'love's sweetest language'.

6

Love : Different States and Stages

God is Love. The human soul, the *Atma*, is a part of the Universal Soul, *Parmatma*, and has the same characteristics and potentialities as *Atma* does, just as a bubble on the water of an ocean is a part of the waters and has the same characteristics and potentialities as the waters do. In the *Atma* is embedded Love—with desire to give and desire to receive.

Love is of several kinds. Mother's love for the Child; Child's love for its parents; Love between brothers and sisters; Love between near relatives; Love of early teenagers for friends of the same age; Calf love; Love of youth i.e. sexual love; Love of the couple at the advanced age; Love of the couple at the old age; Love of Guru and Chella; Love Universal, for the whole creation.

Desire of Love is translated into action like embrace, kissing, hugging, sex, submission of body and mind in the service of the beloved, giving out Love to the whole creation.

Love is desire for Unity. The lover wants to become one with the beloved. Mother holds her child at her arm's length, then brings it to her bosom and presses it against it. She presses the child to her bosom to become one with it.

Embrace, kiss and such a physical contact are expressions of the desire to unite and become one. But the two physical bodies cannot interpenetrate into each other. The physical juxtaposition is the nearest position one can obtain except in the sex union where getting into each other is the maximum obtainable. And it is this union, that is of great importance. Surrendering oneself to the *Guru* is an expression of losing oneself into the Guru. Cosmic love is an expression of becoming one with the created world.

Desire for union runs along the physical channel terminating into sex. As the love gets more refined, only a touch of the beloved suffices. Still later, even this touch is not necessary; the lovers merely want to be in the presence of each other. When one goes out of station, a letter from each other at a regular interval is an assurance of each other's love. Still later, one does not need such a presence or an assurance. The lovers love and that is all. The love between Guru and Chella is Guru giving his grace to the Chella and the Chella his service to the Guru. At the cosmic level, love goes out to the whole creation; it is entirely giving with no thought of receiving.

Love, from the bubbling, exciting stage, matures as the age advances. Kalidas has shown this in *Shakuntla*. Majnu's love for Laila is well-known. Laila was a dark-skinned girl. Friends enquired from Majnu how he could love such a girl. Majnu, replied that one had to look at Laila with eyes of Majnu. God asked Majnu to do obeisance to Him. Majnu felt flustered and said, "What! Do you think you are greater than Laila?" Majnu's love for Laila was very great, but it centered on one Laila only. Higher love would encircle all the Lailas.

As marital love advances in age, there is greater adjustment between husband and wife. Love emanates from each other without desire for physical contact. At the still older age, the two souls seem to merge into each other and it would be surprising to note that even their features undergo transformation and tend to become similar.

It is difficult to describe what universal/ cosmic love is like. There are no words to express the experience. It can only be experienced to know what it is.

This love encompasses the earth creation or at the most, our solar system. But love on a higher level encompasses all the solar system, stars and everything that exists in creation. It is difficult to visualise it. It would be known only when one reaches the Absolute Truth or achieves Godhood.

An average men is conscious of and is concerned mostly with sex-love and love of friendship. This love undergoes many changes and ups and downs, producing pleasure and pain, exhilaration and depression. If one could understand the reason for these psychological changes, it could be easier for one to adjust oneself and lessen the suffering for oneself involved in the changes. These changes occur in every type of earthly love, with some modifications, depending upon various factors. But the basic changes remain the same.

7

Colour in Everyday Life

In life around us, colour is widely spread. It is surprising how little attention we give to it, how little we think of it considering that there is no phase of life where colour does not exist. But perhaps that is natural. A thing that is very intimately connected with our lives, and that is so profusely scattered everywhere is taken for granted. Just as we take our body for granted and do not realise what wonderful machinery it is, and that the most marvellous and the most sensitive and intricate man-made machinery only falls flat before it, similarly we are unconscious of the great and important part colour plays in our life whether physical, emotional, mental or spiritual. In fact, we become conscious of the marvellous working of our body only when we get upset and start losing health.

The use and importance of colour in nature is little realised by an average person. Colour is associated with every phase of life. Colour in nature inspires artists and poets. Harmonious blending of colours is an expression of beauty. Artists express themselves on canvass by means of colours only. Colour is displayed as an ornament on birds, beasts and men. It plays an important part in courtship and amorousness of birds in air, animals and men on earth and vegetable kingdom through the medium of insects and fishes in the sea. Thus nature utilises colour for the continuance of species. Colour is also the cause of germination and growth of vegetable life. It is cause of destruction of insects injurious to human life. It is also a means of protection for the lower and animal life on earth. Worms or insects on the branches of trees are coloured green so that they are not easily spotted by hunters. Animals are light-coloured so that they are not easily spotted by the hunting animals. Colour in nature not only protects insects, birds and animals from being easily detected by the enemy, but the camouflage also gives it an advantage in springing on its prey.

Usually the female of a species has a quieter colour than its male so that she is easily protected from the aggressor whose attention is drawn to the louder colour of the male. Colour also is used as weapon of offence. Some birds have loud coloured pouches which they inflate while encountering another male and this often frightens away the aggressor. Chameleon and a number of fishes have the capacity to change their colour to suit any change in the background.

Colour in flowers attracts birds, bees and insects; they carry pollen from a male to a female flower and help pollination.

Colour has been used to cure diseases, both physical and mental. The constitution and evolution of the heavenly bodies has been determined. By means of coloured lights from those body. Colour has effect upon human mind and thought. Occultists claim to know the extent of physical and spiritual development of a person by the colours of the aura that surrounds him. Colour has created a colour-war between the whites and the non-whites. It plays an important part in choosing our life-mates.

COLOUR AND LIGHT

Colour and light are two different things. Colour is not light, light is not colour. Light is a vibratory motion. Light from the sun emanates in spherical waves, and when these waves impinge on the retina of the eye, vibration is carried to the brain where it produces the sensation of light. If the optic nerve is dead, then any number of waves striking the retina will not be carried to the brain and no sensation of light will be produced. The eye is blind.

When the sunlight is allowed to fall on a prism, light passing through the prism is broken up into seven colours and this patch of seven colours is called spectrum. If this spectrum is allowed to fall on a second prism, the seven colours reunite and form white light. This shows that the white light consists of seven colours—the same as the rainbow does. This can be further demonstrated by a simple experiment. If seven colours are painted in juxtaposition on a round disc of white cardboard and the disc is rotated rapidly on an horizontal axis, the eye will see the coloured rotating disc as white disc. Colours are produced due to the corresponding lights having different frequencies. The frequency of red is much less than the frequency of the violet at the other end and the rest of the colours in between have varying frequencies, increasing from the red end to the violet end. The length of a wave is called wavelength, denoted by the symbol '1', and the rate of frequency of vibration is denoted by the symbol 'n'. All these seven coloured lights emanating from the sun move with the same velocity. The relationship between velocity, frequency and wavelength is given by the equation v = n x 1 (v=nl). Since velocity of the different colours is the same, it is obvious that the wavelength of red light is greater than the wavelength of the violet light. The light of the sun contains wave motions other than the spectrum of seven colours.

Human vision has a limitation. It can see lights only between the red and the violet. This is called the visible spectrum, but there is wave motion beyond the red, called infra-red and there are vibrations beyond violet consisting of ultra-violet, x-rays, cosmic rays and so on. On either side of the visible spectrum, there are a large number of rays. The visible spectrum is only about 1/10th of the whole range of rays in the light of the sun. These invisible rays also must have some colour which the present human eye cannot see. The invisible rays of the spectrum are utilised in broadcasting. Human eye cannot perceive these vibrations or lights; but their existence can be felt by photographic films and other devises. The seven colours are violet, indigo, blue, green, yellow, orange and red (VIBGYOR).

The light of longer wavelengths—red, orange and yellow—are heat producing and are called heat rays or thermal rays. White, green, blue, indigo and violet are cold producing and are called cold rays or electric rays, because they are of the nature of electricity. Infra-red rays are hotter than red and ultra-violet are colder than the violet.

While a human eye can see clearly during the day and not so well at night, the animal eye can see better at night and not so well during the day. It means that though animal range of vision is also limited, it is differently limited than the human eye.

Light is not visible. The sun light coming through the intervening space to earth is not visible. When we look up, we see the blue of the sky and not light of the sun. This can be easily demonstrated by a simple experiment. Make a room perfectly dark, closing all the doors and the windows. Now open the door a little. A beam of light will enter the room. In the beam will be seen a number of particles, floating. These are dust particles. A beam of light falling on these particles is reflected to our eyes and we see light by the reflected light from the particles. If these particles could be removed, we will not be able to see the light. This can be done by placing a source of heat, say a spirit lamp, below the particles. When the particles will get removed from the path of the beam, there will be no light. It will be all dark. Thus light and colour are two different things. Colours are produced by light (wave motion) but they are not the light, just as a blow causes pain but pain is not blow nor blow, pain.

Light is invisible, but what we see as colours, forms etc. is because of light. If there were no light, nothing would be visible to us. We see articles by the reflected light. Light falls on the articles and gets reflected to our eyes and we see the articles. Also we see articles when light passes through them, just as light passes through a coloured glass.

In ancient literature, only a few colours are mentioned. This indicates that in ancient days, human eye could not perceive many colours. During the ages, the human eye has evolved, become more sensitive, and can now perceive more than 2000 hues. There are colours in the astral and the spiritual world which the human eye at the present stage of evolution cannot see. In course of time, through the ages, it may evolve further to be able to perceive these heavenly colours.

An object appears coloured because it reflects that colour. For example, take an object which appears blue. When sun light, which is composed of seven colours, falls on an object, the object absorbs all the other constituents of the sun light except the blue which is reflected and we see the object as blue. That this is so can be easily shown. Ordinary candle light is rich in red rays and deficient in blue rays. If we see a blue object by this candle light, it will appear dark. The candle light contains all the other six colours of the spectrum, except the blue. The object absorbs all the other colours except the blue, so that all the colours united by the candle light are absorbed by it and there being no blue to reflect, no light is reflected and the object appears black. But if instead of a blue object we were to see a red object by this candle light, it will appear brilliant red since there is extra amount of red in the light and red is reflected. Thus an object will look differently coloured in different lights.

Artificial lights are generally redder than the sun light. This is one reason why colour of cloth appears different by day light than in artificial light.

SOME INTERESTING PHENOMENA DUE TO COLOURS

The human eye has in its three chemicals or humours. Each one of them can perceive one colour. The three humours perceive red, green and blue. These are called primary because by adding these three colours in different proportions, any other colour can be obtained. Thus, red + green = yellow; red + blue = magenta; blue and green = peacock blue; strong red + weak green = orange, weak red + strong green = yellowish green; red + strong blue = purple; red + while = pink; red + black = chocolate.

COMPLEMENTARY COLOURS

When combination of any two colours produces white, the colours are called complementary colours. The combination of orange and blue gives white. Therefore, orange and blue are complementary. So also yellowish green and purple; red + peacock blue; green and magenta; blue and yellow.

SIMULTANEOUS CONTRAST

If two complementary colours are kept side by side, their intensity is enhanced. When a coloured object is kept on a coloured background, its colour will appear different e.g. an orange piece of paper kept on a lemon-coloured sheet will appear red. A coloured embroidery will appear of different colour on a coloured background than on a white background. A small white coloured object on a coloured ground will appear to have a colour complementary to the ground e.g. a small white object on a blue background will appear pink, but the effect is lost if the object is surrounded by a black border. This phenomenon is called *Simultaneous Contrast*. Saturation of colour increases when juxtaposed with an area of complementary colour and decreased when the adjoining colour area is similar in hue e.g. yellow appears much brighter when placed next to blue, but seems to fade away when placed next to orange or red.

SUCCESSIVE CONTRAST

There is another interesting illusion known as Successive Contrast. If we look at a particular colour for some time and then turn our gaze to a grey background or close our eyes, we will see a different colour which will be the complementary colour of the first one. Thus if we continue looking at the blue colour until the eye becomes fatigued with it and then turn it to a white-grey background, we will see yellow colour. The white-grey sends all the colours to our eyes, but our eyes being now less sensitive to blue do not get an impression of it, and the sum-total of the impression of other colours is yellow. Hence, we will see yellow. For similar reason, if we look at a picture with chocolate frame for some time and close our eyes, the frame will appear grey-white. Very interesting results can be got by thus fatiguing the eyes. This phenomena was made use of by a manufacturer of a food item in advertising it. A particular shade of peacock blue is complementary to a shade of golden yellow. He utilised this in his advertisement. In a magazine on a glazed paper was written the name of the item in bold letters and in peacock blue colour. A note underneath it said; this food stuff is so good that if one looks at its name and then closes his eye, he will find the name written in letters of gold.

COLOUR AND DRESS

Man dresses not only to protect himself from extreme cold and extreme hot, but also to beautify himself.

Self-display is a human failing, and it can be markedly seen in young people of either sex in the matter of clothes. There are two types of people. One type uses fine clothes for variety—a desire to show off, while the other type is motivated by aesthetic sense—love of beauty, harmony and elegance. They have no desire to show off. Their aesthetic sense, if sufficiently developed, will determine what clothes and what combination of colours will suit them and bring out their personality. The former, as a rule, are negligent and anything but neat and clean. It is this type who needs to understand what to wear and what to avoid.

A dress of the same or similar colours from top to bottom shows no art. Art lies in wearing clothes of different colours in harmony with one another and with one's features, colour of the skin and get up of the body. For example, a pale, anaemic person, wearing a purple dress will only enhance the paleness to a ghastly yellow, and a green dress will bring out the rosiness in the skin. A ruddy person with an orange dress will look better. Coloured garments throw a coloured reflected light on the face of the wearer and produce the desired effect. Each person should find out by trial what colours would suit him or her best.

Various parts of the dress having too glaring a contrast of colours is in bad taste. For example, red and green, yellow and purple, black and orange will produce glaring contrasts. Such contrasts, however, may be usefully employed for theatrical purposes.

Because a particular colour in dress suits a particular individual is no reason why it will necessarily suit another and may be copied, as is often done, resulting in ugliness rather than beauty.

People of hot, tropical regions prefer gayer colours while people of colder climates wear clothes of lighter colours.

Brilliant colours will not look well on persons of large proportions and the aged. They should use sedate colours. Some people, in dress, show great eccentricity. Colours of different parts do not match each other or are out of harmony. In such a case, it may easily be assumed that the person is partly or totally colour-blind. A colour-blind person cannot appreciate colours. He thinks that he has dressed properly, but that dress is out of harmony.

Clothes are not for show only. Attention should be paid to their effect on health also. White or light coloured clothes will reflect more light and transmit less and so keep the body cool, while black or dark colour will absorb more light and transmit heat to the body. Therefore, in hot weather it is comfortable to wear white or light coloured clothes, whereas in cold weather dark coloured clothes keep one warm and cosy.

If a person is cold or pale and bloodless, red or orange underwears and red stockings will make him feel warmer. A person of over-heated, excited nature will find pale blue or lilac underwears comfortable. A person with tendency to constipation or paralysis will find yellow underwears helpful. A light coloured cap or turban will keep the head cool. Those who wear hats will find blue or green lining of the hats restful to the eyes.

COLOUR AND INSECTS

Heat is a principle of reproduction in vegetable as well as in animal life. In summer, heat or thermal rays predominate, thereby helping the growth of insects. That is why, flies and mosquitoes appear in summer. In winter, the cold or electric rays predominate which are insecticidal, and the insects cannot live.

COLOUR IN THE VEGETABLE, BIRD, ANIMAL AND HUMAN KINGDOMS

Colour abounds in the vegetable kingdom. Fruits, vegetables and flowers have a large variety of colours.

Birds show a huge variety of beautiful and brilliant colours. The male has bright colours while the female has dull colours. In the mating season, colour is a means of attracting the female. Sound also serves this purpose. It is the male that sings to attract the female.

Animal, as a rule, cannot appreciate colours with the exception of monkeys. The male monkey has patches of brilliant colours on his body. Also the animal kingdom does not show much colour. The colour of animals is generally dull brown or grey or earthen or sedate. This is necessary for their defence and offence.

Human species has no spectacular colours. Human beings can be represented by white, black, brown or yellow. They make up this loss by artificial means—by colouring the body or by using coloured dresses and by facial make-up.

LANGUAGE OF COLOUR

Colour also has effect on health or emotions or thought. This is well known to the occultists, artists and medical professionals. By observing and noting the effect of colours, it has been possible to prepare a language of colours. From this is derived the language of flowers. For example, poppy flower symbolises purity; amber-imagination; ash—dullness and grossness; black - depression and despair; blue - cooling, soothing, antiseptic, spirituality, devotion in love; electric blue—spiritual; brown - neutral; buff - joyful; clay - deceit, lust for riches; gold - bright yellow - intellectually spiritual, joyful; green - black+yellow - soothing, nerve-stimulating, gladdening, hatred, jealousy, forsaken, forlorn, restlessness; dirty green - fear; dull dark green - jealousy, greed; pale green just before dawn - true sympathy, compassion; Indigo - deep devotion; mauve - depression; orange- sentimentality, soothing, exhilaration; purple - royal splendour, pomp, doleful; red - blood stimulant, exciting anger; blood red - anger; deep red - jealousy; dark red - brutal anger; red and green - teasing; red and violet - abusing; rose - love; scarlet - irritability, noble indignation; streaks of other colours with red-like drops of blood - fierce, impatience; turquoise blue - free of lust or deceit; violet - blood warming yet cooling, spirituality, insult, depression; white - purity, peace, coldness, sterility; yellow - nerve, stimulant, intellect, quarrelsome, joyful, wisdom.

COLOUR—GEMS, PLANETS

Every gem or precious stone emits light of a different colour. Ruby emits light of red colour; topaz emits light of blue colour and so forth. This emitted light is made use of for medical purposes. It is absorbed by alcohol or other which forms mother tincture. From this mother tincture, globules are prepared, as in homeopathy, and are used as medicine. This is called Gems Therapy.

Planets, when examined through spectra-scope, show that each planet emits light of a different colour. A gem emitting the same light is associated with that planet. Ruby corresponds to sun and pearl corresponds to moon. Astrological Kundali shows the position and strength of the planets at the time of birth of a person. It also shows the evil effect or beneficial effect of the planets. In order to mitigate the evil effect or to augment the beneficial effect to a planet, the corresponding gem is taken which should be without a blemish and of a particular size. Pooja is performed on it and is worn in a ring or a pendant or an armlet or in some other way on the body. This improves the material, physical and mental state of a person. Here below is given a table of gems with their English names and the corresponding Indian names, colours of the light emitted and the planets associated with them.

Name of the Gem	*Hindi Name*	*Corresponding light*	*Corresponding Planet*
Cat's eye	Lassania	Infra-red	Ketu
Coral	Mungo Viduma	Yellow	Mars
Diamond	Hira, Hiraka	Indigo	Venus
Emerald	Maratala Panna	Green	Mercury
Onyx	Gomed Gomelka	Ultra-violet	Rahu
Pearl	Moti	Orange	Moon
Ruby	Manka Chuni	Red	Sun
Sapphire	Neelam Indranacta	Violet	Saturn
Topaz	Pukraj Pushparaga	Blue	Jupiter

8
Senses

Man has physical, astral, mental and enlightened bodies. The Ego has surrounded itself with these bodies. It has rather descended from its own subtle plane, through increasingly grosser planes, into the physical or the material plane to gain experience and through experience to evolve. The Devas residing in the Heavens want an opportunity to be born on earth, get into this gross matter, in order to gain experience and evolve. Residing in the Heavens may be quite pleasant, but no evolution is possible there. It is possible only by going through the lowest point of the wheel, the grossest matter. Thus it seems that this physical body is essential for progress and evolution. And evolution is achieved by experience, gained through the physical body.

Our physical body gains experience through the exercise of its five *Gyan Indriyas*, the five senses of perception viz., ear, eyes, touch, taste and smell. These senses of perception move into action the five working parts, the *Karma Indriyas,* viz., feet, hands, tongue, organ of elimination and sex organ. Or, it may be said that experience is gained by the exercise of these ten *Indriyas.* Since these organs of perception and action have been given to human beings, it means that it is necessary to use them for gaining experience.

Hindu religion enjoins *brahamcharya* complete chastity and continence. But *brahamcharya* does not mean control of only sex activity; it means continence of all senses. Complete abstinence of all senses would mean denying oneself any experience and so vitiating the very purpose for which we are here. Therefore, *brahamcharya* cannot and does not mean complete control of sense desires. It means avoiding over-stimulating the activity of the sense organs. It means moderation, check, control so that the Ego may utilize them to gain experience and not lead us to the life of sheer enjoyment of sensations and ultimates to the detriment of the purpose of life.

Since experience can be obtained through the senses, it is necessary to keep them in order and in a healthy state so that they yield correct results and work willingly and joyfully for the ego. This can be done only by giving them constant exercise; otherwise, for want of work they would atrophy or not yield proper results. A judicious activity of senses can alone help attain the purpose of life.

In order to maintain body in a fit state, one needs food. If one does not eat, all senses and organs of the body become incapable of work and the result will be death. Buddha, too, had to realise that austerities not only do not help but positively hinder, and he had to eat what Sujata brought him before he got enough strength in his body to be able to achieve realisation. Therefore one needs must eat. If the sense of taste takes parts in the performance of this act of eating, one enjoys food, masticates better, there is a greater flow of salive, and all this is conducive to better digestion and therefore better health. Again, it is the exercise of this sense of taste that tells us what is good and what is bad for physical health. But if taste gets the better of us and one eats not because one is hungry but to indulge in the sense of taste then the sense becomes a dictator and not a server. Eating becomes an act to get sensation and not an act for the health of the body or for its evolution. In order to *maintain good health*, everything must be done in harmony with nature. One needs to eat only when one is hungry, when the body needs nourishment. Then food produces better results. If we ate absent-mindedly, without our mind in it, just as a matter of routine, and conversely, if we eat to please our sense of taste, we will only overload our stomach and put the digestive machinery out of gear, hurting our health.

Even when food is taken under correct conditions, it is necessary to eat in moderation, overloading results in laziness. Proper proportion is the only true rule. Too much of even a good thing is bad. Water is so essential for our existence, but too much of it will hurt. Poison in a proper proportion acts as a wonderful tonic; a larger dose becomes fatal. An infintesimal homeopathic dose produces wonderful curative effect, but a heavier dose produces just the opposite effect. Moderation, control of the senses to yield the required result, and at the same time to be a source of enjoyment is *Brahamcharya*. *Brahamcharya* is not a kill-joy business. It is, in fact, an increase -joy affair.

What is true of the sense of taste is true of all the other sense organs. Eyes or the sense of sight is for seeing. Unless one uses one's sense of sight, one cannot distinguish between the beautiful and the ugly; between the rotten and the healthy. Sight guides us throughout the course of life. Through sight, we read and write and gain knowledge. Through eyes, beauties of nature inspire and enthrall and turn one's mind to the Creator. But for the sense of sight, culture and progress would not have been possible. Eyes see the beautiful and make one fall in love and love rules the world. But for the sight, love for the beloved would not be possible. Bhakti Marg would not have existed; the sufis and mystics would not have been there. Improper use of eyes leads to passion, covetousness, jealousy, struggle, strife and war.

The sense of hearing makes communication possible. But for hearing, there would have been no growth of language, speech, expression, learning and there would have been no music, no dancing. Music and harmony makes for progress, for evolution. Hearing makes possible bhajan, satsang, puja, ceremonials and a horde of other things. Its improper use - eavesdropping, gossiping, listening to degrading and debasing things leads to trouble.

Sense of touch gives knowledge of heat and cold, of danger. It can also give wonderful happiness. Touch of the loved one is heaven.Touch of the Guru can be a cause of stupendous progress and revelation. Sensation of touch can yield comfort. Yet its abuse can lead to degradation and entanglement with passion.

Exercise of sex is essential for the perpetuation of race and humanity. It is a dominant factor in human life, for the development of culture, for all that is best in life. Saints, yogis, avatars all prophets, did marry, but they did not indulge in the wrong use of sex which converts man into a low beast.

All senses have their use, their need, their necessity. If we are not using them to their maximum capacity as tools for gaining experience, we are only delaying our evolution. But instead of using them as tools. If they are used for gratification, we are working for our degradation. Whenever and whatever we do, if it is done with the help and cooperation of senses, it leads to joy to greater satisfaction. That is, senses help us do things better and with less exertion.

Human being has physical body, emotional body and mental body. His progress consists in gathering experiences through all these channels. Feelings and thoughts get their stimulii from the external, physical world, through the senses. Senses are the tools with which the feeling—world and the thought—world can improve. Senses are the links between the grosser and the finer parts of man. Stimulii through the senses can help man convert or transmute his lower animal nature into higher divine nature. Hence, these instruments need must be maintained in good shape and put to use, otherwise, they will rust.

Desires cannot be killed, nor can thus be suppressed. If suppressed, by the law of action and reaction, they will only rise later with a greater force, often with such a force as to destroy all brakes and will cause a flood. Killing desires would mean destruction of the link between the lower and the higher, destruction of the instruments through which evolution can be achieved.

Nowhere in any philosophy or in any religion or on any land is it advised that desire has to be killed, senses allowed to atrophy. Everywhere it is suggested that senses should not be indulged, that senses and their activity should be controlled to serve the purpose of progress, and that need to transmute our desires to go from the grosser to the refined from animal nature to divine nature. It cannot be done if the senses are killed and the stimulus destroyed. If steam is available, the engine can move. Whether the engine is taken to north or south, uphill or downhill, can be possible only when steam is available. Destroy the steam, no movement is possible

For proper conduct, absolute continence is never advocated; only proper control and use is urged. The four ashramas of the Hindu society are a testimony to it. During the *Brahamcharya* the senses are cultivated and their proper use leant; during *Grahst*, the senses are put to use; during *Vanprastha,* they are used for social service, while during *Sanyas*, they are switched on to spiritual life. Step by step, by proper regulation and study, the activity of the senses is keyed to higher and subtler pitch. The Sikh Gurus have shown the path of evolution while living in the world and *Grahast*. They have not asked the Sikhs to renounce the world.

Brahmacharya is not total continence. No. It is controlled and well regulated use of senses. Sensuality is not an evil; it is a blessing; it is the means of progress, evolution, joy and happiness. Its wrong use is dangerous; it will convert a god into a beast. Choose.

How has woman lost her place in the social life?

Our social life is man-oriented. The man, by virtue of his greater physical brutal strength, has kept woman in subjection. In ancient times, woman was not considered inferior, but during the time that has since passed, man has taken advantage of the circumstances like wars and struggle against neighbouring clans and alien hordes, and has kept her as an instrument for satisfaction of his lust and keep the house for him. Since, the past ages, due to her subjection, she has not been able to take her position equal to man and has, therefore, developed a nature whereby by several ruses and subterfuges, she keeps her man in hand. Knowing her weak social position, she submits to her man, but knows how to twist him round her little finger.

Family doctors say that, after she has had two or three children, she doesn't desire the love embrace more than once a month or once a two months, whereas man's desire does not abate. Woman being in the inferior position as she is today, submits but resents. Woman, in the West, has strongly resented her inferior position and has fought for it to become equal to man. The Eastern woman will not lag behind. It is apparent that in course of time, she will find her rightful position in the society and will know that she is the stronger sex.

9

Truth Behind Mythology

Every society, every culture, every nation weaves stories, fables and myths. Characters in these stories and fables are animals but they behave like human beings, and the moral of the stories is apparent. In a myth, its purpose can be found only by going deep into it. In countries a apart, in the countries in the East and West, fables are similar. In India, *Panch Tantra* gives stories of animals, and *Assop's Fables* of the West are borrowed from the *Panch Tantra*. Surprisingly, even the myths of different cultures are based on the same truths though the stories have local adaptation.

In ancient days, before the advent of writing, knowledge was conveyed from Guru to Chella or from Teacher to Pupil by word of mouth. After the advent of writing, the fables and myths were recorded in books.

In ancient times, teachers accepted pupils if they were worthy of giving knowledge, while those who were unworthy were rejected.

Knowledge is amoral - neither moral nor immoral. It is the application of the knowledge to life that makes it moral or immoral, good or evil. The present knowledge of Electronics in the hands of the wise is beneficial for the human race. It can be used to produce power. It is used in medical service, manufacture of several gadgets for the benefit of man. The same knowledge in the hands of evil persons is used to prepare bombs and other instruments of destruction which could wipe out the entire human race in a few minutes.

To keep knowledge secret from the undeserving, sages gave it by stories, purposely so framed that the undeserving would feel disgusted and run away from it. Whereas the initiated and the knowledgeable would search deeply into it to find out what lies underneath. The stories are so devised that they cannot stand the test of common sense or logic.

A story in one of our *Puranas* says that a king and his wazir went out riding on horses along the bank of a river. After going some distance, they dismounted and sat on the bank of the river. They took off their turbans and threw them in the river, keeping their ends with themselves so that they could pull them out later. There was a heap of salt lying nearby. They took the salt and threw it in the water between the two turbans. The king's turbans had gold thread woven into it and the wazir's turban had silver thread. After some time when they wanted to go back, they tried to pull the turbans out, but they could not do so because they got shocks. They did not know how to deal with the situation. An old woman was passing by. Seeing their predictament, she said she could help them. She brought a wooden stool, sat on it and pulled out the turbans by taking the two ends in her two hands and gave them to the king and the wazir. By all counts this is a silly story. A king and his wazir went out horse-riding in all right. They sat on the bank of a river chatting is acceptable. But why should they have cast their turbans in the water of the river? And why should they have like two urchins, taken up some body else's salt and thrown it in the water? Why did the turbans give them shocks? And what is the sense in an old woman sitting on a wooden stool and handling the turbans without trouble? This may be a good story for a three-four year old child who would not look for logic in it but it, makes no sense when it finds place as a story in our scriptures. But this story does tell us an important scientific truth—namely, how electricity is produced.

In chemistry, all chemical substances are called by a common name *salt*. The story states the basic principle of how electricity can be produced. When a selected salt is put into a vessel of water, the solution becomes a conductor of electricity and is called electrolyte. When two rods of appropriate metals are placed at the two sides of the vessel, they become electrodes - one positive and the other negative - and electricity is produced. If the electrodes are touched, electricity will give shock. This principle is made use of in preparing torch cells and batteries for cars etc.

The two turbans, in the story, containing Gold and Silver threads become two electrodes and salt dissolved in water becomes electrolyte. Wood is a bad conductor of electricity, an insulator. Sitting on the insulator, electrodes could be touched and the turbans retrieved.

The knowledge of production of electricity known to the present day science is only about 150 years old, whereas the story shows that our ancients knew about it long ago and kept it hidden from the common man.

How did the God Ganesh come into being: Ganesh is the son of Parvati and Shiva. One day Parvati told Ganesh to keep guard at the door and not to allow anyone to enter the house because she was going to take bath. Ganesh stood at the gate and did not allow any body to enter the house. Later Shiva came and wanted to go in, but Ganesh would not allow. Shiva argued that it was his own house and Parvati was his wife. But Ganesh would not listen to him. He stuck to his guns and no amount of argument from Shiva mended matters. Shiva got angry and cut off his head. Coming to know of this, gods came rushing to Shiva and pleaded with Him that Ganesh was his own son and was guarding the door at the behest of his mother. They also said that Shiva should appreciate the sense of duty and responsibility exhibited by Ganesh instead of getting angry with him and added that Parvati would feel very much disturbed at the demise of her dear son at the hands of his own father for doing his duty. Shiva relented and told the gods to go about and bring him the head of the first creature they came across. The first creature the gods came across was an elephant. They cut off its head and brought it to Shiva to place it on the body of Ganesh to bring him back to life. It certainly tells a silly story. Didn't Ganesh know that Shiva was his father and didn't Shiva know that Ganesh was his son? And was Shiva so silly as to kill his son for performing his duty? It does not talk high of Shiva's understanding. And again, when he relented, he could have asked the gods to put the severed head on Ganesh's body. In fact, behind this story lies the truth of what Ganesh stands for. Elephant is an intelligent animal and elephant's head stands for great intelligence. Beside, his small eyes can see very far, and his trunk is a powerful organ, and symbolizing great power of the God. The pot-bellied body means that Ganesh can swallow the sins and the troubles of his devotees. Thus the God Ganesh stands for an intelligent entity which can see very far, and has great power to take on the sorrows and troubles of his devotees.

Once gods were discussing as to who was the greatest among them. Ultimates, it was decided that the gods, riding their vehicles, would run the race of circumbulating the earth and he who completes first and reaches the starting point first will be considered the greatest of them all. The vehicle of Ganesh is *Mouse*. He wondered how he could run the race when vehicles of all the other gods moved faster than his, the mouse. He remembered people saying that he who worshipped his father and mother and parambulated them seven times, was considered to have parambulated the earth. He want to his father and mother, Shiva and Parvati, worshipped them and went round them seven times. The other gods running the race found foot prints of the mouse ahead of them. They were puzzled. How could a mouse go faster than them? They moved faster and still faster, and yet found the foot prints of the mouse ahead of them. Thus Ganesh was the first to complete the race and was declared the greatest among them. In Sanskrit, the word for mouse is the same as for *time—Mooshak*. The real meaning of the vehicle of Ganesh is *time* and not mouse. Ganesh never procrastinates and does things always continuously. He does not waste time. That is why he is the first amongst gods and is worshipped at the beginning of any function, be it a birth ceremony or a marriage or commencing building of a house or a factory. On the symbol of Ganesh *Swastik* is added, at its four ends a little curve which gives the impression of the symbol revolving, that is moving fast. It also symbolizes completion of the undertaking quickly.

The four *Vedas* are supposed to have desended from the heavens. The text of the *Vedas* was conveyed by word of mouth by the sages to their disciples. During the days of the *Mahabharata*, the Muni Krishna Dwaipa thought it was time to commit the *Vedas* to writing. He looked for a scribe who would be suitable for the purpose. He hit upon Ganesh and requested him to take dictation from him, to which Ganesh agreed with the condition that he would not halt while writing and that dictation should be continuous. Krishna Dwaipa composed 99 verses and dictated them to Ganesh. The hundredth verse was made difficult so that Ganesh took time to understand it. During that period, Krishna Dwaipa composed another 99 verses. The *Vedas* were written on the bank of the river Indus. Krishna Dwaipa came to be known as Veda Vyasa - He who had mastered the *Vedas*.

It is said the Kam Dev, the god of Love, has five arrows in his armoury with which he wounds the hearts of human beings and embroils them in love. Embedded in the human heart are two strong instincts, one of self-preservation and the other of self-perpatuation. Self-perpatuation means raising progeny. Desire for love is ingrained in the human heart which is excited by sensual impressions, gathered by the five sense organs viz. Eyes, Ears, Nose, Taste and Touch. These five senses are the arrows of Kam Deva. The eyes see the beauty of the beloved, ears hear her voice, nose feels her smell, mouth has her taste and touch brings excitement. During the spring season, the cool breeze excites the desire of love; smell of flowers excites the desire; the moonlight excites romance in one's heart—poets have gone crazy over moonlight and have even compared the face of the beloved to the face of the moon. The story that when Kam Deva wanted to excite Shiva and take him out of his Samadhi, Shiva opened his third eye - the eye located between the two eye brows - and burnt him up. This shows that when a person has reached the Spiritual stage when the fifth Chakra or the Chakra between the eye brows is activated, he acquires the power to control his senses and conquer passion.

Devas & deites - gods and demons - the spiritual forces and the material forces - are always quarelling among themselves and struggling to have supremacy over each other.

These forces decided to churn the ocean to get from it what they could. A mountain was made the spindle and a snake the rope. Demons held the face-end of the snake and *devas* held its tale and the churning of the waters of the ocean started. *Nine Ratans* were got from the ocean, amongst which was a pot of *amrit* and a pot of poison. *Amrit* is life, poison is death. Both the *devas* and the demons wanted *amrit* only. The *devas* caught hold of the pot of *amrit—Kumbh* - and ran away with it. As they ran, some the *amrit* spilled. Some of the poison also got spilled. Poison being deadly, it had to be kept away for the life—giving *amrit*. They wondered where to keep this poison. Shiva offered to keep it in the throat. It is because of this poison that Shiva's throat became blue, and that is why he is called *Neel Kanthaya*, i.e. Blue throated.

What is the thought behind this story? *Devas* represent the positive or the Spiritual Principle and *demons* represent the negative or the material principle. These two principles are struggling for supremacy. Ocean represents life, snake represents time, demons - the material forces hold the face-end of the snake, while the *devas* - the Spiritual forces - held the tale-end of the snake. Material forces want to keep man in the material world, while the spiritual forces want to take him out from materialism to spirituality. Progress in life, evolution, will come by struggling to ward off material forces and moving towards spiritual forces. Progress is not possible without this struggle. It is only when troubles, obstacles, handicaps arise that man struggles to get over them. It is just as in the obstacle race where participants struggle through the obstacles to win the race. Thus the cause of struggle is always the impediments put forth by the material forces. The commencement of the struggle is due to the material forces or the Demons, and the end-result is evolution, success, the triumph of spiritual forces - the Devas. Life exists in time. The churning of the ocean is the struggle. Since the commencement of struggle is due to the material forces, the face-end of time is held by the Demons. And it is only by churning, struggling, that precious objects or evolution is achieved.

Life, to start with, is neutral, On churning it, it gets separated into its positive and negative aspects - Amrit and Vish - Nectar and Poison. Amrit and Vish are equal in quantity. Since it is so, why should man act or do anything in life? In order to act, man needs some incentive i.e. pleasure should be greater than pain. Otherwise, life will come to a standstill. The *amrit* spilled was slightly more than the Poison spilled, i.e. in life, pleasure is slightly greater than pain.

A child wants to learn to stand and run. While learning, he falls down and often hurts himself, but he does not give up, because the pleasure of being able to stand and run is greater than the pain of falling and getting hurt. When he learns to run, he feels very happy, as if he is on the top of the world.

A woman bears a child and delivers. This is very painful, but the joy of having a baby of her own and giving it love and getting its love is greater than the pain. She supports the pregnancy knowing its pain and pleasure.

Parents try to provide for their children. They make them comfortable and happy and give them schooling and education to make them fit for life. In doing so, often they have to forego their own comforts. The pleasure of seeing their children well-off, is greater than the pain of depriving themselves of their comforts.

To get freedom for India, several freedom fighters sacrificed their lives. They gave up their good jobs, went to jail and suffered beatings at the hands of police. Their families suffered economic hardships. All this was very painful, yet they accepted it because the joy of expectation of freedom was greater.

Persons who are doing social service honestly and sincerely have to face many difficulties, but they accept all this willingly, because the pleasure of serving the community is greater.

Examine any action - moral or immoral, ethical or unethical, right or wrong - and it will be found that this action is motivated by the thought of finding pleasure. No action would be possible without this incentive of pleasure. As a matter of fact, life would come to a standstill and creation would disappear if this incentive of pleasure was not there. Life has been possible because of the sacrifice of Shiva, who kept the poison or a part of the pain of humanity in his throat.

There is a vast store of stories and myths in our literature - Puranas and folklore - underlying which are the truths of life - philosophical, psychological and material. Studying and delving deep into them will bring out what heights of intellect and culture our ancients achieved.

10

Brotherhood—Its Meaning and Purpose

Science is the study of the laws of material world. Philosophy is the study of the spiritual worlds; Religion is the application of Science and Philosophy to life. Looking at a problem from different angles and co-ordinating the different views gives an integrated picture which goes a long way to solve problems - individual, social, national and international. A philosophy which a social unit accepts colours its culture and evolution. That is why, from time to time, Nature has thrown up reformers, preachers and prophets to direct the evolution of portions of humanity. Different portions of humanity develop along different lines and then intermingle and thereby enrich the culture and accelerate human evolution. These changes don't take place overnight; they take long periods of time; but the pattern is clear to the students of the history of human evolution.

India, long ago, as a credle of Aryan culture, gave the pattern along which the Aryan culture was to proceed. Portions of humanity - India, Persia, Babylon, Asyria, Egypt, Greece, Rome and now the West, developed some definite traits, for example, Persia emphasised purity; Egypt occultism; Greece art and beauty; Rome polity; the present West liberty. From India the inspiration travelled westward. Time after time, people from the West came to India for the purpose of learning, trade, conquest... to drive inspiration and be coloured by its culture and in the process to colour the Indian culture. Time has now come when the peoples having developed along different directions must come together, pool their experiences and hammer out an integrated philosophy of life for the whole human race. The guiding forces of Nature seem to be working in that direction and are creating conditions for its fulfilment. Science has shrunk time and space of this earth and efforts are being made to do the same for our solar system. An overwhelming desire for an integrated human philosophy is being manifested. Its practical shape will be Universal Brotherhood.

Theosophical Society, some eighty years ago, realizing that the time for the brotherhood—phase of humanity was approaching, gave a call and introduced it as one of its objects. The thought took on. Nature threw up forces at different points and Communism, UNO and a horde of other organisations sprang up to propogate brotherhood of man. Now the idea has caught on and peoples of different ideologies accept this as an Ideal, though they differ in their approach to the ideal.

Currently, hot disputes are going on regarding the right approach. This conflict is also a necessary part of the change or evolution. In course of time, the conflicting views will get adjusted and an accepted approach will be evolved. A great, indeed a very great, experiment of brotherhood of man is being initiated and organised. It would be exciting to watch the progress of the experiment and to contribute one's mite towards its success.

The ideal of universal brotherhood has been so much talked about that it has percolated to the level of the man in the street and is being easily accepted as the right thing. This attitude of easy acceptance is a necessary concomitant to the success of the experiment; but it would be infinitely more helpful if the common man was emotionally and mentally convinced of its desirability. Then he could and would take an intelligent part in this experiment and greatly accelerate its pace. Mere faith can falter, but faith based on conviction can stand as a rock, and it is such a faith that is essential for the success of an experiment at the level of humanity. If everyone was convinced of the necessity of achieving this ideal, he would work for it with devotion, with the spirit of a crusader. He will then know that in every walk of life, in every incident of life, in the daily conduct, this has to be practised and he will know how to do it.

Before universal brotherhood can be accepted as a philosophy of human life, it is essential to appreciate its necessity and usefulness on different planes of human existence—material, moral, intellectual and spiritual. What, therefore, is the answer to the question: "Is this ideal of universal brotherhood necessary, feasible, practicable? Is it or could it be the wish of Nature to have universal brotherhood?"

For the first part of the question, let the economist, the politician, the statesman and the philosopher answer, and they have answered in the affirmative by creating several agencies to work for this realisation. For the second part, let us look around and see how Nature conducts itself and what lessons it teaches and what directives it gives.

Looking at life, we find it to be a continuous, perpetual struggle and strife. The sea is for ever trying to knock down the earth and swallow it. Wind is always lashing at the sea and life on the earth. Fire is ever out to destroy and consume what is touches. Larger birds prey on smaller birds; smaller birds devour insects and worms; insects eat away vegetation; birds eat up vegetable life. Stronger animals live off the weaker ones. Carnivorus animals prey on the non-carnivorus. Herbivorus animals consume vegetation. Even individuals of the same species—bulls, monkeys, dogs as also the birds—fight unto death with one another over food and love.

At the human level, life is no better. Individual fights against individual, community fights against community. Nation fights against nation. Race fights against race. Selfishness and not service and sacrifice is the law. Human history is the history of struggle, strife and war. At the present moment, the same state of affairs obtains on the international chess-board. The *Ramayanan*, the *Mahabharata*, remind us that even in the hoary past, this state of things existed and the Divine avatars - Rama and Krishna - took part in it.

Where then is Brotherhood and Equality? Nature does not seem to be in favour of brotherhood. In fact, it is opposed to it. It believes in struggle, destruction and death.

Is Brotherhood then against the law of nature, a mere fancy of the human mind, a will-o-the-wisp?

The object behind the French Revolution was to establish liberty, equality and fraternity. It did nothing of the sort. Communism started with the ideal of downgrading aristocracy and upgrading proletariat to create one-class society: equality. It hasn't succeeded. If there were equality, there would be no incentive to progress, there would be stagnation. Railway, aeroplane, rocket, bomb, interplanetary travel and a lot more is the result of competition, struggle, fear, hate, jealousy..... Cosmologists and evolutionists tell us that progress results from struggle: survival of the fittest. History of human progress is the history of progress of human fight and war. The keener the struggle, the greater the progress as witnessed during the last two centuries. If they is to be believed, then surely this is an emphatic vote against Universal Brotherhood - Liberty, Equality and Fraternity.

So?

We have been listening to arguments based upon incomplete premise, and have therefore, arrived at incorrect conclusion.

Mankind cannot be equated with the sub-human life. In fact, no life can be equated with another. Minerals cannot move of their own accord; they require an outside force to move them. They have one-dimension awareness. The vegetable life though rooted at one spot, can move only to and fro and has two-dimension awareness. The animals can move about freely, possessing three—dimension awareness. Man is midway, with three sub-human natural regions below him and three super-human or spiritual regions above him. He is the bridge between the material and the spiritual. In Man Nature has, for the first time, achieved a new dimension, that of awareness of self. Man, thus, occupies a unique position in the scheme of Nature and cannot be considered at par with the lower, material life.

The sub-human life acts by instinct, it haven't developed reason. It has no mind or creative impulse. There is no change, no progress in any species. Since time immemorial, gold has remained gold; there has been no change in its physical, chemical or electrical properties. And so have other minerals. Wheat has remained wheat; mango has remained mango. Donkey has remained a donkey; lion has remained a lion. They have not changed in their characteristics, habits, temperaments or features. In spite of fights between members of the same species, or fight for existence between different species, through the ages, they have remained the same.

Nature has its own way of maintaining its economy. By making one species instinctively prey on another, Nature controls their numbers as also achieves several other purposes. White ants cannot co-exist with ants. Mice vacate when cats enter. Disease germs and insects are destroyed by other germs and insects, and so on. Law of the jungle is Nature's method of maintaining its economy as also achieving results in its experiments.

But it is different with Man: There has been progress, sometimes slow, sometimes rapid. To the new generation, people of a previous generation look out of place, physically, emotionally, intellectually, and culturally.

Man has reason, intelligence, mind, the creative power which the sub-humans do not possess. At the human stage, for the first time, has man become capable of being conscious of self, so that his progress consists in the development from the lowest to the highest consciousness, culminating in self-realisation. At the human stage, self-consciousness exhibits itself as will, wisdom or activity, so that the human evolution consists of sensual perception, control of senses and awareness of self. Or, what may be described as: domination by desire, conflict with desire and control of desire. This brings man to the brink of self-realisation when he glides from the material region into the region of the spirit.

These three aspects of awareness are factors which can raise man to godhood or downgrade him to the level of animal.

Desire impels man to get at the object of desire. Pain and pleasure teach him which desires to maintain and which to drop; what objects of desire to strive for and what objects to discard. Mind and wisdom give him knowledge of good and evil; and by discarding evil and accepting good, he builds his character. By activity, he can create circumstances and environments which can help in the achievement of the first two objects. Thus, man has freedom and power to create which the sub-humans do not have. Hence, man is different from the sub-humans and has different capacities, responsibilities and purpose.

To realise the purpose of his being, man has to struggle against the material or satanic or "Asuric" powers which hinder and obstruct spiritual evolution. This opposition is the very nature of matter which is characterised by inertia and resistance to change. This resistance is an essential factor to make progress or evolution steady and durable. This is illustrated by the mythological story in the Bhagvat Purana, of churning of the ocean by Devas and Asuras. It is only by chruning—struggle between the advancing and the retarding forces—that ratans (jewels) could be obtained.

In order to achieve God-realisation or Self-realisation, man has to realise oneness of life - Unity of Life. Brotherhood is a step in that direction.

Religious teachings, throughout the ages, have also pointed to brotherhood of man. All philosophies, all religious are agreed on the point that there is only one God. Logically, if there is only one God, He must be the same God, though named differently by different prophets and peoples. Then all men, whether born in one religion or another, with white, brown, yelllow or black skin, are His children, children of one Father, and therefore are brothers.

Again, a child born anywhere in the world, whether in Asia or Africa, Europe or America, inherits a physical body, emotions, intellect, character, capacities, capabilities..... from his parents; and these characteristics have been developed by the effort of thousands of generations of human beings before them. Thus, every child is the inheritor of the accumulated wealth of experience of the human race through the countless generations. The sum-total of the experience of the whole human race is pooled and passed on to the new-born generations. Therefore, all children are the children of humanity and as such are brothers. And each child, as he grows into manhood, has individual and collective responsibility to the one family—the humanity.

Also, we see that life in practice runs or cooperative basis and not on individual or separatist basis. Family life, group life, community life are all based on cooperation. So in the life of a nation, the administrator, the politician, the builder, the destroyer, the general, the dictator or the democratic head, all derive their support and power from the collective will of the people of a country. This is a collective responsibility. Whether the nations of the world will live in peace or be plunged in struggle and strife depends upon this collective decision. The right or wrong decision will affect not only the present generation but the following generations as well. It is, therefore, sheer common sense and self-interest that we exercise our individual and collective responsibilities wisely, in the spirit of brotherhood, so that not only my unborn child but all the unborn children of Man may have something better to be born to; and, also, we may justify our own existence. What hurts the whole, hurts each component; what benefits humanity will benefit my child too.

The humanity is being torn as under by fear, anger, jealousy and hatred. Not only this state needs to be counter-balanced, but a positive state of cooperation and understanding also needs to be established if humanity has to survive and not to go the way of Lemuria and Atlantis. Understanding, forbearance, patience, charity and affection flowing out of brotherhood is the way.

Brotherhood connotes liberty, fraternity and equality. What do these terms stand for? There can be no physical or economic equality. No two things, in the scheme of nature, are equal. No two leaves of the same tree are equal. Children of the same parents are not equal - they differ in looks, in character, in capacity and in talent. Even the parents do not love their children equally. Equality is an attitude of the mind. A brother may be low-witted or poor or afflicted, yet the better-placed brother's heart will go out to him. The brother belongs to the family and is accepted as 'mine'. Equality consists in this attitude of 'accepting' the other as 'belonging'. From this will follow the equality of opportunity. No one shall be shut out because of race, religion, sect, sex or colour from striving and achieving a position in life. Success will be by merit. Liberty is liberty of mind and thought. No brain-washing, no compulsion, no restraint beyond that prescribed by society for the proper conduct of social life. Fraternity means brotherhood. Thus Brotherhood translates itself into sympathy, understanding, affection and service.

Caste and class were bulwork of social stability in the previous ages. But Vedas and scriptures say that this system of caste and class will not be practicable in Kaliyuga; that in Kaliyuga there ought to be only one class and man shall worship the same deity, the one God. This is a divine command or prophecy. So, Brotherhood is on the book; we have scriptural sanction; we shall be wise in ushering it in.

Further, character-building is the first step on the spiritual path. To control Tamas and Rajas, and increase Sattva in every day life, is the *sine qui non* for an aspirant. And what better way can there be then the practice of brotherhood!

It is a herculean task. Habits of thought of long standing do not change overnight. We have arrived at the present sorry state of things by wrong behaviour through centuries. Destruction is easier than construction. Human evolution is slow and it will take generations before brotherhood becomes the key-note of the new civilisation. But that need not deter us; in fact, that should goad us to take to the task quickly and earnestly. Seed has to be sown before a tree can grow and bear fruit. If every one does his bit, starts adjusting his individual life to conform to the brotherhood pattern, we shall have lived purposefully.

11
Ahimsa

Ordinarily, by Ahimsa we understand 'don't kill'. If a bug bites you, don't kill it. Let it suck your blood. In some sects, they go so far as to let a man lie on a cot having bugs and give them a feast of his blood. If a snake attacks you, let it do so. If a dog bites you, allow it to do so. To save germs from getting into your mouth and so getting destroyed, the mouth and nose is covered by cloth. Not only should one not kill, let oneself be the object of attack by parasites. This is what Ahimsaites preach and endeavour to practise. But is this possible and is this the real meaning of Ahimsa?

If we read our scriptures, puranas etc., we find them full of wars between the Devas and Daityas. They go on destroying each other. Rishis, at the slightest pretext, curse and destroy. Lord Krishna brought about the war of Mahabharata and the destruction of his own clan. Lord Shiva is the God of Destruction and, is the greatest Himsaic personality. How then can we be asked to become Ahimsaic?

Look at life as it is. From our birth to death, continuously we are in for destruction. Child in mother's womb lives on her and off her. He is parasite. Born, he lives on her milk i.e., on her life blood. When he grows, he eats grain, fruits, vegetables and meat, and all this is destruction of life. Not only have animals life but all plants also have and by cutting them and eating them, we are destroying life and being guilty of Himsa. We drink water and breathe in air. Both these things contain myriads of micro-organism which we destroy and become guilty of a large-scale murder. We wear clothes made of cotton and silk. We must destory cotton shrubs and silk worms before we get clothes. Our shoes, whether of leather or cloth, mean killing of animals or plants. At every step, we have to kill and destroy. If

Ahimsa has to be the law of our life, then the only logical conclusion is that we should not eat and should not wear clothes, drink no water and breathe no air. But then this means suicide or self-annihilation which again is Himsa.

If an army of locusts comes to destroy our crops, shall we or shall we not destroy them? If we don't destroy them, they destroy our crops and so starve us to death. If an enemy army invades our country, shall we not fight? If we don't, they will kill, murder and loot us. If there is a disease, shall we not destroy the offending germs? If we do not, the disease will spread and destroy us instead. Either way we become agents of destruction.

Look at Nature. You have been lizards swallowing moths. Larger birds, the birds of prey, attack smaller birds. Carnivorous animals prey upon the gentler animals and take them for their meal. Larger fish live off the smaller ones. Waters of the sea are lashing against the land and swallow it up. Air is always grinding off the mountains. Look anywhere and you find nature always destroying. The birds, the animals, the fish, all have no sense of morality. They are immoral. They destroy because nature has imbedded this principle of destruction in their nature. They do it by instinct. They are not to blame. A child is always destructive. Give him anything. He will break it, destroy it. Killing and destruction is in the very nature of our being, implanted there by mother nature. How then can we be Ahimsaic! If practice of Ahimsa is suicide, that too is negation of Ahimsa. How can we get out of Himsa? It all looks so absurd and impossible.

Man, in the earlier stages of development, lived a nomadic life. Clans moved from one place to another. Clans fought each other for food and law of the jungle prevailed. We are now more organised, but this organisation rests on Himsa or the threat of Himsa. There is Military and Police to protect us from the bad, the criminal elements by use of force. Courts are symbols of punishment. The whole organised life has force or fear of force as its basis. We would be attacked and swallowed by others if they were not afraid of greater physical force. Our homes and our possession would be unsafe, if there was no fear of punishment.

Rani of Jhansi is esteemed because she was out to destroy the British. Rajputs are considered great because of their physical prowess which meant destruction of the enemy. Rama is great because he destroyed Ravana, and Krishna's greatness lies on the field of

Mahabharata. You all know the story of Panna. She got her son killed in place of the Prince and we extol her.

Yet, is this principle of Ahimsa given to us by our philosophers, by our yogis, by our scholars, by our great ones? Surely, they could not be a pack of fools. They could not be so absurd as to preach something that is impossible of achievement. Does it not, therefore, seem that perhaps we have not quite understood the meaning of Ahimsa?

Himsa means killing, hurting or injuring. This also includes emotional and mental injury. One may not kill, but can be emotionally and mentally cruel. In Europe and America, there are cases of divorce on the ground of mental cruelty. Thus Ahimsa should mean avoiding injury by act, word and thought.

But we have to use these also as instruments of correction or for development. If a child misbehaves and if he does not alter his conduct in spite of love and affection and sympathetic correction, it becomes necessary to use emotional or mental screw-tightening. It would be criminal not to do so. The fear of punishment is necessary to keep man from aggravation. Thus, the only conclusion we come to is that Ahimsa means no wanton destruction—whether physical or moral, emotional or mental. We have to use Himsa or force when and where necessary. If it can be avoided, it must be avoided. But if it can't be, then it must be used. Viewed in this light, the laws of Nature would appear benevolent.

Life in the vegetable kingdom is of a low order. In insects, it is a little higher. In animals, still higher, and in man, very much more so. If in order to preserve and develop human life, we have to live on and destroy vegetable life, it is not Himsa. Pasteur experimented on animals to help man. Every time we exercise our body, we destroy cells in it. We eat to create other and better cells and so grow and develop. If lower life is destroyed for the preservation and development of higher life, it is no Himsa. Nature is continuously destroying the old to build the new, and the new is better. God incarnates to destroy the evil and re-establish righteousness. What, therefore, this should mean is transformation, and if the transformation is for the better, it is progress, it is good. Change is the law of life, and change means death of one thing and birth of another. God has a plan of evolution. Anything done to help evolution is spiritual; anything done to hinder it is sinful. Hence any injury or use of force or killing done wantonly means Himsa.

Wrong idea of Himsa and Ahimsa has cost India dearly. In ancient India, surgery of a very high order was practised. Even brain operations were performed. Plastic surgery was common. Certain crimes attracted cutting off of nose and ears and these organs were artificially replaced by plastic surgery. Plastic surgery was performed by barbers even as late as the time of East India Company of England. Surgery involves cutting and opening of the diseased parts, and this they started calling Himsa. Little by little, it fell into disrepute and disappeared. It is only about 200 years back that some young people defied public opinion and learnt and practised surgery. We have had to import surgery having lost our own. Surprisingly, the instruments used in surgery today are similar to those used in ancient India. The marauding hordes that came to India to loot us, took advantage of this idea of Ahimsa. They put rows of cows in front of our forces and the Hindu soldiers would not use their arms against them. Thus the marauding hordes won the battle with hands down.

The Sanatan Dharma is a militant religion. The mantras chanted during 'Sandhya' invoke that we become strong and our opponents and enemies be crushed and destroyed. The wrong understanding of Ahimsa emaciated the Indian nation and India lost its freedom. The Western world laughed at our imbacility—that a few hundred Britishers were ruled over millions of Indians.

Self-protection and self-preservation are the two instincts, basically ingrained in man as also in animals and birds. Self- protection and self-preservation by any means do not constitute Himsa.

12
Religion and Religious Philosophies

The great religions of the world are of two types: those that recommend renouncing the world and taking to monastic life—like Jainism, Buddhism—and those that want their followers to live in the world, fulfil their duties and not to shirk them, and so living, understand life and attain moksha—like Hinduism, Christianity, Sikhism. Fleeing the world is cowardice. Living in the world, struggling against environments and facing odds is manliness. To this type, renunciation comes in the end when reality has been realized. One cannot but renounce that which is unreal, that which is but a shadow. Perhaps both paths secure bliss, but there is a difference. Bliss of the renouncer in vacuous in character—it is the bliss of the type—"When ignorance is bliss, it is folly to be wise", whereas bliss obtained after living and understanding life is alive, all-inclusive, throbbing, and pulsating one.

All prohpets, all messengers have come from the same source, the same one God, to guide and reveal a facet of the truth to the erring, straying humanity. Different messengers have revealed different facets of the one reality or sometimes the same facet is re-revealed in a different way to suit the understanding of the people of that time. Therefore, it is reasonable to accept the least common factor of the teachings of all the messengers throughout the ages. But if someone wants to find the truth for himself, he can well do it. The knowledge exists. The knowledge that the ancients, our ancestors, gathered also exists. 'Unconscious' is the collective store-house of the universe. If the seeker follows the path, he will ultimately discover the truth by himself. He need not rely on what is 'told'. But that what is 'told' may inspire him and spur him to greater effort.

Each society, each race, each country, has developed in accordance with its environments, and this has brought about so many differences. For example, West extols animal energies in man while East counsels mastering animal passions, with the result that philosophies of life of the two people become very different from each other. These are, in fact, superficial differences which are capable of modification on change of environment. Sympathy, goodwill and understanding is necessary to rise above these superficial differences, for ultimately, man, in whatever part of the world, is the same. The least common factor of humanity is the human soul, and knowledge of the soul i.e. spiritual knowledge, can build bridges to connect all men and realise the brotherhood of man.

13

He and She—Purusha and Prakriti

Life on earth began millions of years ago. Starting from a simple organism it evolved through large number of organisms till it reached human form. Some of the creatures have disappeared and some remain. Human foetus in the mother's womb goes through several stages of evolution, resembling forms which exist in nature, till it reaches the human form in the fifth month of pregnancy.

From mono-cellular organism it has evolved to become multi-cellular organism. Human form contains millions of cells. An example of mono-cellular organism is amoeba. Amoeba consists of a single nucleus and protoplasm. It grows to a particular size, then becomes narrower at the centre till it snaps into two, each part containing half of the nucleus. Each half becomes an adult so that uni-cellular amoeba becomes two units. Every new unit again divides and becomes two. Evolving through ages, a multi-cellular organism had positive and negative elements in it and these two principles inter-acting with each other gave birth to progeny. This is symbolised by the picture of God Hari Har. It shows a human form, the right side of which is depicted as male and the left as female. Still later, two sexes were separated and procreation resulted from the meeting of the two. This is symbolised by the story that Lord Shiva, getting angry, cut off the head of Prajapati. The gods and sages pleaded with Shiva that if Prajapati died how could the race be proliferated? Shiva relented and told the gods to go about and cut the head of the first creature they came across and place it on the body of Prajapati so that he would alive. The first creature the gods came across was a goat. They cut off its head and placed it on the body of Prajapati who become alive. Goat is a sexy animal and is a symbol of sex. Thus Prajapati, with the goat's head, meant that thereafter children would be born by the union of two sexes. At this time, evolution had reached a stage when children were to be born by the co-operation of man and woman.

Man and woman were created with difference in their physical form, mind and emotions. They are both complementary to each other. Functions and responsibilities of the male are different from those of the female. They must both co-operate for the continuance of the race. They form two wheels of the same chariot or two wings of the same aeroplane. Both have equal status and usefulness.

POSITION OF MAN AND WOMAN IN NATURE

Life consists of two forces: positive and negative, spirit and matter, Purusha and Prakriti. All the creation has been created by Prakriti. All forms of life or all that is created is created by Prakriti. When the positive principle or the Purusha permeates the forms created by Prakriti, life comes into being. This is two principles working together. Purusha, the positive principle is the giver; Prakriti, the negative principle is the receiver—she is the receptacle. It is the co-operation of the two that is life.

Evolution had reached a stage when Prakriti decided to separate the two sexes and the propogation of the species was to be carried out by meeting of the two sexes. The sub-human species instinctively seek their partners during breeding seasons and relieve their biological urge. The human race was also to propogate by union of the two sexes. Humans were given mind and thereby got freedom of when, where and how to meet, while the sub-human species meet only during their breeding season by instinct. The human race was given greater freedom of action and made responsible for its Karmas. The love embrace in humans is not only a union of the physical bodies but also union of two minds and two souls. In this ideal meeting, the two lose their consciousness of separateness—they become one like what happens when you pour milk in a pot from two bottles in two hands, when the two streams mingle and become one and indistinguishable. This is the ideal condition as the Prakriti wants it to be. Such a couple will provide a human body fit to be incarnated by a highly developed soul. The ecstasy experienced in such a love session compares well with the ecstasy experienced by a Yogi in his Samadhi.

Guru Gorakh Nath and Gargi Devi were discussing various problems. Gargi asked him a question on sex. Gorakh Nath replied that he was Brahamchari and had no experience of sex and pleased for a period of six months to experience it and then to reply. At that time, a king was dying, Gorakh Nath ensouled the king's body. The king became alive and Gorakh Nath lived marital life in the physical body of the king. He was surprised to find that there was a tremendous ecstasy in the physical union. Rather he would not leave the body till he was retireved by one of his disciples.

Man gets his spirituality direct from God, while woman gets it from man through sex. Thus has God ordained. Milton expresses this truth when he says: "He for God alone, she for God in him." Also Manu, the law-giver, has decreed that woman consider her husband as her lord and master, and worship him as her god. In this lies the salvation of both. The spiritual truth behind this is that Prakriti or Matter can come alive only when spirit pervades her. Man is not aware of himself until he pervades woman. It is like engine and steam: engine without steam is so much junk; steam without engine to work through is so much waste. The co-operation of the two produces motion, creates life. Manu has also prescribed rules of conduct for the male so that he becomes worthy of worship by woman, as he has prescribed rules of conduct for woman in order that she becomes an ideal partner in the production of human race. He has further said that in a house where woman is not respected and not considered as Lakshmi, that house is like a burning ghat.

According to him, the attributes of man and woman go as follows:

She is Language; he is Thought.

She is Prudence; he is Law.

He is Reason; she sense.

She is Duty; he is Right.

He is Author; she is Work.

He is Patience; she is Peace.

He is Will; she is Wish.

He is Pity; she is Gift.

He is Song; she is the Note.

She is Fuel; he is Fire.

She is Glory; he is Sun.

She is Motion; he is Wind.

He is Owner; she is the Wealth.

He is Battle; she is Might.

He is Lamp; she is Light.

He is Day; she is Night.

He is Justice; she is Pity.

He is Channel; she is River.

She is Beauty; he is Strength.

She is Body; he is Soul.

The present-day man has lost this perspective and is behaving like an animal wanting to just relieve his biological pressure. It will be useful to understand why and how this has happened, and find remedial measures to achieve a perfect union as wanted by Prakriti.

FALL AND RISE OF WOMAN

In the present-day civilised world, woman runs after man. She decks herself, uses make-up, goes semi-dressed, adopts changing fashions and employs other ruses in order to attract him, to get him and to hold him. Why does she have to do that? Woman is the custodian of new life, she is the preserver of life and culture. She is already fulfilling a difficult task. Now why should she go about hunting for a male? This does not sound reasonable. There must be something wrong.

In the insect world or the realm of the birds or the kingdom of animals, it is the male that is more beautiful, more colourful, songster and stronger. All the beautiful colours of the bird world belong to the male. The dance belongs to the peacock; mane is given to the horse and to the lion; crown is the glory of the cock; glow comes from the male glow worm, and all the beautiful music from the bird world is provided by the male. The male is so equipped because it is he who has to court and win his lady-love. By his glittering colours, he seeks to attract her. By his dance, he endeavours to dazzle her. By his music, he tries to excite her. And if there are rivals, he fights them, vanquishes them and establishes his prowess before the lady. The female's colours are generally dull and drab. Can, then, things be different with human beings?

At the earlier stage of human evolution, man lived in groups to hunt for his food and protect his belongings, and the groups moved from place to place. As members of such a group were blood relations, any sex relationship within the group was prohibited. Hence, male of one group would go with presents and offerings to a neighbouring group and woo a female of his choice. He would perhaps pass the night there and in the morning get back to his own group and to his work. Children of the union lived with the mother and the mother's group.

Time came when the male wanted his mate and his children to live with him and go wherever he or his group went, according to the exigencies of time. This was a difficult problem. In those far off uncivilised days, as also now in aboriginals races, it was the woman who did the hardest and the most tiresome work besides bearing children. As such, she was a very valuable member of the group and the group did not like to part with her. The wooer, therefore, in order to compensate the parents for the loss of this valuable worker, would work with his son-in-laws for a stipulated period, or give them oxen or horses or any other useful object as a compensation or as the purchase-money for the bride-to-be.

With the progress of civilisation, easier conditions of life, division of labour, machine doing the work of human beings and woman's work at home has become less valuable. Milking the cow, preparing food, laundering, tailoring etc., is now being done by others and her value has depreciated in the ratio of her usefulness. Even her value as a fruitful mother is at a disadvantage, because children only mean so many more mouths to feed, so many more parasites. Woman's purchase-money value declined not only to zero but parents had to give compensation value, in the form of dowry, to the would-be-groom for taking care of her. And even then, perhaps, one half of the marriageable woman of the civilised world do not find mates. The result is that now it is she who has to run after the male and practise all sorts of lures instead of the male running after her, as he did in the past.

The fall of woman is due to her less usefulness. She can regain her status if she learns to make herself increasingly more useful. Even today, a woman who has succeeded in securing a good earning position is sought after. She therefore, must develop sufficient self-respect not to be a commodity for barter. She must know that the man's need for woman is much greater than woman's need for man. It is always a male that fights for the possession of the female—whether in the human kingdom or the animal kingdom or the bird kingdom. Sparrow is a house-hold bird, and everybody notices that he is chirping all the day to please and attract the female and wants to mate with her a number of times everyday. The male scorpion approaches the female with trepidation. If she is not in a mood, he turns tail and runs away. If she is in a mood, they will lock their four arms, dance for a while before they mate. Similar is the case with other living creatures. If the woman can hold out, she can subdue the man and bring him to his senses. Female needs physical protection and security of home. Man has greater physical power and, therefore, he can be a protector. Formerly, woman was economically dependant on her husband. Now the woman has potential economic independence and even if she is not a working girl, the male works outside and earns and she keeps home to make him comfortable. It is interdependence. No one can do without the other.

WARNING TO MAN

Eve was the cause of downfall of Adam. She got him and herself ejected from the Garden of Eden. Adam suffered and Eve too had to suffer and struggle alongwith him. But does she really suffer? She enjoys it—because the material world and the mesh that is life in her fulfilment.

How does woman hold her man?

God gave her qualities, attributes, beauty, magnetism to attract man. How can iron resist being drawn to magnet? This attraction results in progeny. The child is dearer to her than he who gave her the child. She now spreads her web wider and tighter; she goads him to labour harder to keep and support her and her offspring. He works to acquire food, clothing, house, comfort and luxuries by hook or crook to satisfy her insatiable desires, cravings and whims. He gets so involved in things material that he strays from his origin; loses his spiritual heritage and willingly accepts the bondage that is woman. He thinks he does it out of love. Woman is Shakti, Prakriti, Maya, Matter, the female aspect of the creation and it is her function to create and entangle. Life comes into being only when Spirit, the male principle, pervades matter, the female principle. She fulfils her being only when Spirit enters. into her. Lord Krishna used to sit in meditation. Arjuna enquired to know on whom did the Lord meditate and why did He have to do it when He Himself was God. Krishna replied that His meditation consisted of trying to prevent the encroachment of Maya, as Maya was very strong and would invade Him as well if domain of Maya and is surrounded by her power.

No true discipline, philosophy or religion can ask man to flee the world, shirk his responsibilities, be a coward. Life consists of world of matter as also of spirit. We need to partake of both, but in proper proportion so that the material forces do not dominate the soul and make it lose its contact with the Spirit. Man will then be no better than a beast. Enjoying the life of the world, man should remain master of the material forces, of the desires of the senses and be progressively in greater contact with the world of Spirit, because to reach godhood or self-realisation is the goal of our existence. Sooner or later we have to do it because the "Hound of Heaven" will not let us alone.

Man needs to live a life of Dharma - Artha - Kama and Moksha. Living according to the social law and custom (Dharma) let him obtain worldly things to live comfortably (Artha) and be able to fulfil his desires (Kama) and then strive to become detached from them so as to obtain freedom from them (Moksha). That is the path prescribed by sages so that man can have the best of both the worlds. If man is master of himself, woman will be of help for living such a life and not be a hindrance. It is only when man loses himself that Maya dominates him and keeps him embroiled in its web.

WHO IS THE WEAKER SEX—MAN OR WOMAN

Ours is man oriented world. Man is considered stronger sex and woman is the weaker sex. Yet man has been warned against woman throughout the ages. Sages, social reformers and others have warned him against her. He has been told to beware of her not to get entangled with her, not to run after her, as she will pull him down into the mire. On the other hand, man has subjugated woman, tyrannised her, ill-treated her. She has been driven by the ill-treatment of her husband and his people to commit suicide. She has been used as vehicle as an instrument to satisfy his passion. She has been treated as a mere serf.

But, it is by the union of the two that a new life commences. For procreation, woman is the instrument of nature. Woman, after receiving from man, conceives, gestates, delivers, feeds and brings up the child. For all these duties, she has to be well-equipped. Her body is more complicated, more delicate, more sensitive than man's. Emotionally, she is better equipped. She has implanted in her the mother's love. She can stand pain and physical strain better. She has greater sense of love, beauty, service and self-sacrifice. Mentally also, she is well equipped and there is a suspicion that she is better equipped than man. This is borne out by the fact that in the examination results, girls are often the toppers and a working woman in various branches has shown that she is equal and even better than a man in a similar position. In fact, as for the qualities of head and heart, woman is better equipped than man. Man is superior to woman only in physical, brutal strength. Nature, in her wisdom, has given man greater physical strength to serve her purpose. Man's function, after giving the positive principle to the woman, is to protect her, give her a home and food, as also to the offspring. Beyond this, nature has no use for man. In the honey bee group, ordinary bees are the workers. Only the queen bee procreates. There are drones, the male bees. When the queen bee is ready, she leaves the comb and flies high up. The drones, a number of them, that are in the comb, fly up after her. She flies higher and higher. Those drones that cannot go so high, get exhausted and die and fall. One that can reach her, impregnates her and dies immediately after. He is wanted no more. The queen bee returns to her comb and is taken care of by the worker bees. Similarly, nature has no further use for man after he impregnates the woman. The only function for him is to protect her, give her a home and provide for the offsprings—something that the workers bees do. Woman's superiority has also been recognised by the sages. They, as also the Gurvani has said, "Gurdev Mata, Gurdev Pita." Mother is the first Guru or the teacher, the father takes the second place.

14
Karma and Destiny

Buddha says: Deep indeed is the Law of Karma. It is by not knowing, by not understanding, by not penetrating this doctrine that the world of man has become entangled like a ball of twine... unable to pass beyond the way of sorrow, and ceaseless round of births.

Mrs. Besant says: Karma is the ultimate law of the universe, the source, origin and fount of all other laws which exist throughout nature. It is the unerring law which adjusts effect to cause on the physical, mental and spiritual planes of being. As no cause remains without its due effect from greatest to least, from a cosmic disturbance down to the movement of your hand, and as like producers like, Karma is that unseen and unknown law which adjusts wisely, intelligently and equitably, each effect to its cause, tracing the latter back to its producer.

Mahabharat says; Just as fruits and flowers come to the trees at their appointed time, unimpelled by anyone, one's past Karma never transgresses its appointed time.

Karma means cause and effect, action and reaction, to which all human conduct is subject. Newton's third law of motion, viz. every action has its reaction which is equal and opposite, applies as much to moral law as to the law of physics. Law of Karma is also a law of compensation. It is inexorable spiritual law from which even the highest gods could not escape. Dharampada says: Not in the sky, not in the midst of the sea, not if we enter into the clefts of the mountain, is there a known spot in the whole world, where a man be freed from his deeds. Vishnu, Dasrath, Ravana, Parikhshat, Krishna, all had to pay for their Karma.

Karma is primarily mind created, but it acts on all the three planes, the mental, the psychic and the physical. It takes place in three ways; (1) It recoils on the doer. A harmful action, when directed to another person, boomerangs on the perpetrator, (2) It results in retribution. A man given to over-eating, may be borne with a weak stomach; (3) It acts in a symbolic way. A man shedding the blood of an innocent may be borne with a wasting disease like anaemia.

In the realm of Karma, none is ever made to face more than what he can bear.

Freedom and Karma are two aspects of the same reality. We are, all the time, making our own Karma and thus determining the character of our next birth. Our destiny is in our hands or rather our character is our destiny. Man has a free will but what he does will remain with him and bring him return.

Nobody can prevent the working of 'prarabadh' and, therefore, there is no use thinking much about it. 'Sanchit' (present) can be kept in good stead by incessant striving—it will create 'prarabadh'. This process of 'sanchit' and 'prarabadh' goes on continually from birth to birth.

Chistman Hemphreys, in his book, 'Karma and Rebirth', says: All that we hate and despise in the acts of others we ourselves have sometime done, and paid for, or, are paying now. The treatment you get now reflects back the treatment you have given to others. An act of kindness returns to you as an act of kindness. An act of cruelty comes back to you as an act of cruelty. A great mind which has abused its body may be born with a poor body. A glorious body, carefully nourished, but with a vicious mind reflects the visciousness in the face. Cruelty can result Karmically in blindness or anaemia, asthma or paralysis. Sexual excess can result in epilepsy. Selfish thwarting of others can result in the paralysis of one's limbs. A man cannot press the life out of others without seeing at times to have it pressed it out of himself. So, one should learn to live and let others live.

The writer knows a lady from a very high family who was practising spiritual discipline. Her whole body had patches of leukoderma. She remained unmarried. Discussing the subject, she said that this state of her physical body was a punishment for her transgressions in her past life. In her previous life, she was a beautiful woman, highly sexed and became a prostitute. This ungainly physical body of this life is a punishment and expiation of the transgressions of the past life. She died at a ripe old age and hoped that the present discipline would help her progress spiritually in the next rebirths.

A friend told of a dog in Hardwar. The dog would do 'Shastang Dandvat' to the rising sun, bathe in the river Ganges and then take food, if offered, or go out in search of food. Evidently, this is a case of an advanced soul reborn in a dog's physical frame for some transgression or evil Karma, which he is expiating in the present life of a dog.

Many more cases could be cited.

For cessation of Karma and for one's final salvation, the Gita prescribes disinterested action. When the mind is disinterested, Karma does not touch it and it puts an end to the cyclic reactions set off by one's action.

Disinterestedness does not mean lack of interest. It means lack of *selfish* interest. It means lack of selfish attachment. One should not become passive and avoid Karma to escape the responsibilities of life. For, those who do not actually work for the betterment of others, commit sin of omission and those who consciously exploit others commit a sin of commission.

No blame is attached to rising waters producing floods, or to storm causing damage or to fire consuming valuables, because water, air or fire have no enemity with man and their actions are not the result of any evil intentions. The function is accordance with the laws of nature and are not held responsible for the result—good or bad. Similarly, if man acquires self-realization and acts in accordance with the Divine Plan, his actions do not affect him; he is not subject to the fruit of his actions, neither good nor bad; he is not subject to the law of Karma. Man comes under the sway of the law of Karma only when he is living within the domain of the pairs of the opposites. Beyond this duality, Karma does not operate.

We talk of destiny as something inevitable, something beyond our control; as if we are slaves and victims of destiny. We attribute good as well as evil things in our life to our Kismet, to our Karma. And that becomes the final word in any discussion on the matter. If destiny is as important as that, if it is such a powerful force, there is all the more reason that we should know as much about it as possible in order to control it. Whenever man comes across a force, whether it is water or air, electricity or atomic, he goes out to learn more about it and does not rest till he knows a good deal about it, at any rate enough to control it, bend it to his will and press it into service for his own comfort and progress. Then why not know about this force called 'Destiny'?

Destiny and Karma go together. Destiny is the result of our Karma. We therefore, need to know all about Karma—what it is, its laws, the method of its operation, etc.

Karma is one of the fundamental tenants of Indian thought and culture, the other being reincarnation. Destiny and Karma form part of other systems of thought also; only they do not lay so much emphasis on it as does the Hindu thought. Islam talks of Kismet; Christ's illustration of the blind man is there. Heaven, Hell, repentance and sacrifice occur in all the religions and all these are the direct result of the doctrine of Karma. Again, direct consequence of Karmic Law is Reincarnation which no religion, no philosophy, modern or ancient, has not accepted, albeit with different amounts of emphasis.

In order to know how to control our destiny, it is necessary that we know Karma that produces destiny. We need to know what constitutes Karma and how we can regulate and control it.

Now, all knowledge can be got in one or all the three ways: direct perception (Scientist), influence (Philosopher) and testimony (Teachers or Prophets). We can make use of all these three ways to understand the problem of Karma.

Karma means action. Science tells us that every action has a reaction which is equal and opposite to action e.g., pressing the wall; hitting and pain. Action is the cause, reaction the effect. This cause-and-effect take place according to definite universal laws.

Now, to save anything from burning, cover it with asbestos; to save yourself from the electric shock while repairing electric installations, you need to stand on a wooden plank or some non-conducting material; to go on smoothly in your office, you need to please your boss and do what he wants you to do; to get God's or Guru's grace, submit your ego to Him.

Action on our part is brought about by the activation of our senses. Since we cannot lock up our senses—and if we could, there would be no life—it means we have to act. If we have to act, we have to suffer reaction. Then what is the way out? In order that all reaction or effect be pleasant, one needs to know all the laws. This is an impossibility. But then it is not necessary to all the laws. One does not know all the laws of the land and still never has been hauled up for not knowing all the laws. Some fundamental laws we know; and whenever there is need to know some special law, we consult a lawyer and find out about it. That is exactly what we need to do to make our destiny pleasant. We need to know some fundamental laws and for any special law, we can consult those who know or refer to the written word.

The fundamental law is Evolution, the fulfilment of the divine plan. If you go with the plan, with the stream of life, you are on the correct path. Go against it, willingly or unwillingly, and you are in trouble. No one on the level of human evolution can know the whole plan. One can only find out or determine one's own place in the fulfilment of the plan. No employee in an organisation knows the whole plan of the office work except the supreme boss. Yet, everyone is doing his limited piece of work that goes towards the fulfilment of the whole. The General alone knows the whole plan of strategy during a war. He orders different units to do different pieces of work. He sends some to sure death... Viewing his orders individually, one would call him a fool, a cruel fellow.... But he knows the plan and achieves its fulfilment.

Everyone has, by his action, determined his destiny. His body, his parentage, his environment is the result of his Karma. And the present environment has been adjudged by the Masters of the Law to be the best for his working out the effect. As such, one should make the best of it. It is no use saying that given opportunities, he could have done better. His environment is just what was correct for him.

Poverty, nagging wife, defective children and tyrant boss—they are not always meant to create trouble for us. They may be there just to teach us adjustment, tolerance, fortitude, responsibility...

All that is transitory is unreal and illusory. That which is permanent is real.

15

Garden of Eden

God decided to create. He created minerals, plants and animals and then He created Man. He created man in His own image, with creative faculty and desired him to be His co-worker in the field of creation.

According to the Book of Genesis (Fall of Man), God told Adam that there was the world of mineral, plant and animal life for him to organise, control and develop; that in this task he would be guided by God Himself and that he should always listen to the voice and direction of God. He was also told that if he did so, he would have no trouble; his food and other necessities would be made available to him and that he shall not have to labour for his sustenance.

Then to provide Adam with company, as also with complimentary qualities, God created Eve for him.

To accomplish their work, Adam and Eve were given instruments and powers—the senses, heart and mind. They were told to restrict themselves to the task assigned to them and not to go beyond it, not to dabble in the how, why and wherefore of the mineral, plant and animal worlds. With the instruments and powers provided, they could venture in those fields, but they were specifically ordered not to do so and not to eat the fruit of the forbidden tree of knowledge.

Adam, and later Adam and Eve, both worked together diligently in accordance with God's guidance and plan, according to His will, and were very happy doing the work assigned to them. They organised the world, and as time went by, they remained engrossed in their work, but they were carried away by their success, and in her enthusiasm, Eve, being inquisitive and nosy, desired to know the why and wherefore of things. She prevailed upon Adam and made him transgress the Divine orders. They started eating the fruit of the forbidden tree. They did not wait for God's guidance; they forgot to listen to His voice and got lost in the joy of achievement. In fact, they forsook God.

But they did not have the necessary knowledge to carry on their work. They got lost in the maze of Maya. Finding that their work was not proceeding smoothly, they indulged more and more into the mysteries of matter.

God felt displeased with them for using their will instead of His will, and told them that if they considered themselves as capable of running the world by themselves, they could try, but they would be responsible for what they did and would have to bear the consequences of their handiwork. He, then, turned them out of the Garden of Eden and placed an Angel with a Flamming Sword at the entrance of the Garden to prevent them from entering it.

Thus was man (Adam and Eve) condemned to eat his bread by the sweat of his brow. That is, he could not know and gather knowledge, material as also spiritual, by his own efforts, by struggling and suffering.

Adam and Eve in their blindness, in their ignorance, in their intoxication, heeded Him not. They made a mess of things and got embroiled in the mesh of their own making. Instead of keeping the animal, plant and mineral power under their control, little by little they came under the spell of their power—they became the ruled, instead of being the rulers.

By transgressing the Divine order, by using his self-will, did man fall a prey to the material or lower forces or what is called the Satan and his hordes. And in order to be able to re-enter the Garden, he had to encounter the Angel with the Flaming Sword. That is, before he could re-enter the kingdom of the spirit, he had to destroy his lower nature, extricate himself out of the power of material forces and keep them under his control. Then again could he able to listen to the voice of God and working according to His plan.

God, in His infinite love and mercy did not forget man. From time to time, He has sent Messengers to remind man of his origin, his work, his destiny. He has been told, as for example, Krishna said in Gita, that man must dedicate his action to God and not look for its fruit, i.e., man must once more learn to listen to and act according to the Voice of God. When man learns to do so, he will regain the paradise have his destiny fulfilled.

Hindu philosophy says the same thing, though in a different way. God created man and sent him forth to experiment with and gain experience through the material forces. All philosophies more or less, agree that there are seven planes of existence and corresponding degrees of consciousness. The seven planes are the planes of Spirit, Soul, Wisdom, Human, Animal, Plant and Mineral. Man, starting from Spirit, descends into matter and then again ascends back to the Spirit. The first part of the journey consists of the descent from Spirit into matter, the going forth, the Evolution, where man uses his self-will. The second part consists of ascent from matter to Spirit, the path of return, the Involution, when man gives up his self-will and accepts God's will. The two-way journey constitutes the whole circle of Life—from Spirit, back to Spirit—from the Garden of Eden, back to the Garden of Eden.

Ancient Indian writings tell us how, in those ancient days, kings and others could hear the voice of God—Akashvani—and how they could recognise the messengers of God, who would walk into their courts and give them guidance, which was thankfully received and acted upon. But as man got more and more steeped in the material life, this faculty got lost and man could no longer hear the voice of God or recognise His messengers. That is why Christ was crucified and other messengers were not recognised and understood.

This history is repeated in the life-story of every human being. When a child is born, it is in communion with its soul and with spiritual powers. It is common knowledge that a child, after taking birth, experiences states of joy and sorrow, pain and pleasure for which there is no apparent cause. These states are due to reaction of contact with the soul and higher powers. At it grows and its senses develop, as it learns the use of limbs and discovers its own mind and learns to have its own will, its contact with the spiritual forces decreases, till it is entirely lost. So long as it is a child, it is in communion with God, and all its needs are fulfilled by the mother and is well served. But as it grows and exercises powers of its own senses, mind and will, the free service decreases; It has to exert itself to satisfy its wants. And as it grows into manhood, it has to work to supply its needs. It has to struggle and suffer and eat its bread by the sweat of its brow. Sometimes, there is one who realises its plight, frees it from the clutches of material forces, re-establishes its contact with God and is he saved, to re-enter the Garden of Eden.

When Adam and Eve ate the fruit of the forbidden tree, they discovered their power of procreation. To start with, the children born were spiritually inclined. But generation after generation, as man came more and more under the spell of the material forces, the children born were materially minded, so that, step by step, man strayed farther away from Godhood.

Man is the vessel that contains the seed; woman is the vessel in which the seed is nurtured. Medical science tells us that the physical, emotional and mental conditions of the mating pair, at the time of mating, have a profound effect upon the child conceived. Also that the feelings, emotions and thoughts of the mother, during the period of gestation, have a telling effect on the temperament of the child. Thus, the state of mind and the nature of the pairing couple is an important factor in determining the type of the child conceived. If the pairing couple, before pairing, adjust their feelings and thoughts and during pairing turn their mind to God, the resulting progeny will be better equipped to carry out the plan of God and, in course of time, the humanity can regain the lost paradise.

Man is capable of understanding and controlling with his mind the three lower forces viz., mineral, plant and animal, while the higher three—Roohani, Rahmani and Rabani—are beyond the ken of his mind. His mind can neither know nor understand and explain them. This knowledge could be understood only by his Soul, and that knowledge can come to him only by God's grace—as a gift. He cannot get at it by his own effort, his own will or the exercise of his mental powers. God's grace can descend upon man only when he has conquered and subjugated the lower forces in himself and stilled his mind. This is Death before the actual physical death. This death is the liquidation of the lower forces in man. At this, death is man born to the higher spiritual forces. This is what is symbolised by the death and resurrection of Christ.

All true philosophies, all true religions, all true spiritual disciplines, aim at the same thing—conquering the lower forces and stilling the mind. Purpose of concentration and meditation is to quieten the mind, to check it from constant activity. It is only the blank mind that can receive the Divine guidance. Mind withdrawn from the sensual pursuits and desires, mind unaffected by the wind of the lower forces, can alone receive the grace of God. Free Masonry also teaches the same thing when it says that the Mason must re-discover the lost secrets at the centre of the circle.

Mystical literature talks of 'Death' before the physical death. 'Death' does not mean the killing of the material forces in man or destruction of senses—the instruments of perception of the material existence, it only means death of their dominance in man, putting these forces in their proper place for use in the worldly life, because they are needed for man's physical and material life and well-being.

Nor does resurrection mean man's giving up the worldly life and taking to *sanyas*. Resurrection does not preclude worldy life. If man is to renounce the world, how will he carry on God's work or organising matter? How will he experiment and gain experience of worldy life. While living in the world, man can and is required to live the life of the Spirit. No prophet, no messenger, no true religion advocates the renunciation of life of the world. Krishna, Christ, Nanak and others have taught us how to live the life of the Spirit while living the life of a house-holder.

In spiritual and mystical literature, the expression 'ferry across the ocean' occurs often. A Guru, a guide, ferrys a disciple across the ocean of material life. It means that a Guru helps his disciple who is ready, who has learned to be unaffected by the sensual passions, who has learned to still his mind, receive direct contact from the Divine Spirit and, thereafter, conduct his life in accordance with His will. Several instances are recorded at different places.

Once Guru Nanak met a businessman who surrendered his all—body, mind and wealth—to the Guru. The Guru, thereupon, asked him to do something and the businessman did not reply immediately. The Guru asked him as to what he was doing. "Thinking", replied the man. The Guru said, "How can you think? One thinks with one's mind. You have surrendered your mind to me. You cannot use that which you have given away". The businessman understood what the Guru meant—the real surrender of mind and stop thinking. And he was ferried across, so it is recorded.

One of the Sikh Gurus once proclaimed, that he who can recite the Japji Sahib in his presence, one-pointedly, without allowing his mind to wander, will get whatever he demands. One Sikh was confident that he could do so, and commenced reciting the Japji Sahib. His mind remained quiet and he recited the Japji Sahib without any disturbance from his mind. As he was about to finish, he wished that the Guru should give him his beautiful horse as a reward. The Guru read his mind and announced that though he was so pleased with the performance of the Sikh that he was about to confer *moksha* on him, yet since, at the last moment he wished to possess my horse, I give that to him. The Sikh lost a rare opportunity because his mind or rather his desires were not entirely under his control. In other words, he was not ready for the Divine contact.

It is said that Raman Maharishi disliked anyone touching his feet. He also discouraged talking and would ask his visitors to sit quietly in his presence, and he himself would go into *samadhi*. While in *samadhi*, he would be working on a higher plane trying to help his visitors control their minds and so help them progress towards a state where direct contact with the Divine could be had. Talking and asking him questions would have been working on a mental plane which he discouraged. Several friends have experienced that in his presence, their mind was stilled and the questions they wanted to ask him looked foolish and the difficulties they felt before reaching him seemed to have dissolved.

It is a common experience that in the presence of a Real Spiritual Being, one's mind is stilled. One feels a deep calm. In fact, this is one of the tests of a person being a person of high Spiritual attainment.

Here is where the need of a Guru comes in, which is so much emphasised, at least, in India. The two-way journey of a soul is from Individuality, consisting of the three spiritual forces, into Personality, consisting of the three material forces. Since ages, man has been affected and dominated by the lower forces. In order to master, regulate and utilise these forces, need of a guide or a Guru is essential. Little by little, step by step, the Guru will teach and guide and lead the disciple from darkness to light. Personality has not be destroyed, it is to be put in its proper place and made use of. Reality will be realized by the Individuality and man will realise that Spirit and Matter, Positive and Negative, are only two sides of the same coin of Reality.

16

Why Reincarnation?

Reincarnation is the basic doctrine of Hinduism and the whole Hindu culture has been moulded by it. In fact, reincarnation doctrine exists in almost all the religions of the world. Great men, whether philosophers, scientists or poets have accepted it. Great religions of the East include reincarnation as a fundamental tenet. In India, as in Egypt, reincarnation was the root of ethics. Pharisees held the belief "the virtuous shall have the power to revive and live again." In ancient Greece, Plato and other philosophers taught reincarnation. Neo-platonists held this belief. According to Paracelsus and Pythagoras: all is soul, all is soul wandering in organic world. Ovid, Boheme, Swedanborg and others taught it. For Romans, it was proclaimed by Gicrdano Bruno and Campanella, and is referred to by several poets. Egyptian civilization was built on some crude form of reincarnation. According to them: human soul is imperishable, when a man dies, his soul enters another creature—human or animal—that may be ready to receive it. Belief in the existence of soul after death gave rise to pyramids and what is found in pyramids, and the articles kept alongwith mummies point to this belief.

Christianity accepts reincarnation. This belief was prevalent in the days of Christ and the doctrine was taught by the church upto 6th Century A.D. In new testament occurs that John the Beptist was the reincarnation of Elijah—and this was confirmed by Christ. Again, disciples asked Jesus regarding a man, born blind whether he was suffering from the sins of his parents or for sins of his own. Zohar speaks of souls being subject to transmigration. Jacob was loved before he was born; Esau was hated before he was born. Jeremiah was proclaimed a prophet before he was born. Again salvation and damnation, atonement and sacrifice, heaven and hell have absolutely no meaning if there was no life before the present one, or if there was to be no future life. Love, sacrifice, service, repentance make no sense at all. The belief was common in the early Fathers of the church and they preached it. The christian scriptures point out as revealed truth that man shall live after death, that he came into being with the birth of the body, created according to the will of God, in a way and with a justice incomprehensible to man. Ancient christian writers like Origin believed that 'God did not make men suddenly as they are, but ordained that every man born into the world received the deserts of his former actions.'

During the 'Dark Age' in Europe, this belief was considered as heresy by the bigoted, and due to religious tyranny, this truth, along with several other truths, was lost. But with the passing off of the Dark Age, the best thinkers throughout Europe have advocated it. Max Fuller has said that Reincarnation is a belief held by all the greatest minds that humanity has produced. In Germany, Schopenhaur, Hegel, Leibnitz, Herder, Fichte, Kant and others have accepted it. In England, Cambridge Platonists advocate it; Henry Mare, Hume and others believe in it. American and English writers and poets Sir Arthur Conan Doyle, Lessing, Emerson, John Mensefield, Robert Browning, Walt Whitman have believed and expressed their belief in their writings. In America and Canada, millions of people have come to accept it—so much so that reincarnation plays have been put up; and many clergymen are preaching it from the pulpit. The doctrine is accepted as essential teaching of Christ.

Northmen, Gauls, Druids, the Celtic peasantry of Ireland and Brittany; Red Indians of America; Eskimos, Zunis, Incas, Hawaiins people, Australian natives, South Sea Islanders believe in it. Chaldeons, Jews, Arabs, many Mohamadan Sufis, Talmud and Cabala teach it. It is the fundamental principle of the religion of Persian Magi. Negroes and many tribes of Africa accept it. All teachers have taught it and these teachers knew what they were talking about. Buddha taught it and knew his past 500 lives. Tao, Orphews, Pythogras taught it.

Thus it is the fundamental religious idea of the overwhelming majority of mankind. Endurence of the idea for thousands of years, since the beginning of mankind, shows that there is some truth in it, otherwise it would not have endured for so long. But Hinduism alone gives the most scientific explanation of the doctrine.

In the 19th century, idea of evolution influenced the thought in Europe, and in the twentieth century Reincarnation is influencing the thought of the Western World. East has never doubted it.

There is a good case for reincarnation as a rational explanation of life. It makes us understand several problems of life. It is the only explanation to what science calls evolution. It is necessary to the progress of morals, ethics, intelligence and to the divine justice. It solves so many problems of our life, gives us dignity and purpose to live for, and ideal to strive after, something to aspire for and make a beauty of our life.

It explains phenomenon of growth and decay of nations; different capacities of individuals; recurring cycles in history; different human character.

Agnosticism is the direct result of refuting the tenet of reincarnation, because to the agnostics, it would otherwise appear that God is a capricious power who distributes favours according to His whims, who is devoid of all human pity and sympathy, who is inhuman, lacking all human feeling; such a God is not worth accepting.

A future life based on whims and caprices and tyranny of God is not worth having. It would thus seem that there is no such thing as God; there is Devil who enjoys the pain and trouble of man. This would, thus, be a contradiction of what scriptures say about God, that He is all Love, Mercy and Justice.

WHAT DOES REINCARNATION MEAN?

The purpose of reincarnation is to train the animal-man to become a perfect instrument for the Divinity to work through him and the Reincarnating ego is the agent to do this piece of work, to train the animal-man.

The doctrine says that the world around us has invisible regions, that the man's subjective nature exists objectively in those regions as a *Soul;* that this soul survives the death of the body and that the soul, the true immortal man takes to himself, time after time, a body and so evolves throughout the ages by repeated incarnations in earthly bodies by gaining experience. He gradually becomes stronger in Will, Love and Knowledge, the divine qualities. These states of hell and heaven are neither dull nor fearful. They are temporary.

Sri Krishna has said in Gita that it is the body that is slain and not the real self.

It is the fifth principle or the Thinker or the Soul that reincarnates. It incarnates in the animal-man to gain experience which he accumulates, remembers and uses. The animal-man, the physical body, has never been born before and has no past. It is fresh and new. The gain of experience belongs to the Thinker and not to the body. The body is only an instrument that the Thinker uses to gain experience. The richness of the experience depends upon the capacity of the brain of the animal-man; the more perfect it is, the greater the experience and the greater the evolution.

THE PROCESS OF ACQUIRING KNOWLEDGE

All knowledge can be obtained in three ways; inference, direct perception and testimony. All these methods presuppose faith; faith in the laws of nature and the laws of thought, faith in one's own senses, and faith in the judgement of others. These three categories of search after knowledge produce philosophers, scientists and religious teachers respectively. And all these categories have accepted the doctrine of reincarnation.

WHY DO WE NOT REMEMBER OUR PAST

Physical brain is not the seat of memory. It is only a receiving and transmitting instrument. We note an incident, or see a scene, or hear a music—external vibrations, through our senses, produce vibration in our brain which produce the appropriate sensation of seeing or hearing or testing or smelling. The cause of vibration is external to our brain, but the brain vibrates in unison and produces the impression, just as a radio receiving and receives vibrations from the transmitting station and passes them on to the listeners in the room. The origin of music is external to the radio. But all that the brain receives is recorded in some subtle part of man and whenever, under suitable conditions, that record is excited, it, through the brain brings back the same scene or music and this is what we call memory. It is something like a gramophone record of a singer's voice. Under suitable conditions, we can hear the song over and over again though the singer himself is not present and may be dead. The gramophone record is the memory of his voice. Often a suggestion brings back to us memory of a forgotten incident; playing of a gramophone record brings back to our memory a whole, vast scene where we had first heard that song. But a huge lot of incidents in our lives we cannot remember, even if we earnestly try to remember. If brain were the seat of memory, there should be no difficulty in recalling any incident of our life, howsoever trivial it might be.

How, some incidents leave a strong impression on us and others leave just a scratch. Those that leave a strong impression can be recalled easily from the store house of memory, while those that are weak, fail to be recalled - just as a weak sound is not heard from the radio-set. The brain is always in a state of activity, it is always vibrating. If an impression of an incident is strong, its vibrations overpower the normal vibrations of the brain and get themselves felt and so we remember; whereas the weak impressions produce weak vibrations. They cannot assert themselves and we cannot remember them. Just as when there is an atmospheric disturbance, the vibration of a song do not get through the radio. But if the activity of the brain could be stopped, the weaker impression also can get through and any and every incident of our life can be remembered. That this is so is demonstrated by hypnotism. Under a hypnotic spell, the physical brain is asleep. It is a inactive, its functioning is stopped, with the result that the memory of the medium becomes very much sharper and the memory of forgotten incidents, of babyhood, is easily recalled. But on removing the spell, the medium remembers noting, not even the fact that he was hypnotised. He is blank regarding the incidents during the period of the spell. Thus physical brain is not the seat of memory.

Again, a hypnotised person can be made to see things that do not exist for a normal individual, or things that do not exist materially, they exist only in the thought of the hypnotist. This would show that the physical brain is not even a repositary of knowledge. It is only a channel for transmitting knowledge. The real record is elsewhere which is not visible to our physical senses. Hence, we infer that there is an invisible world around us, and that record is in this invisible world.

Light and colour do not exist. One gets an impression of light and colour through the sense of vision, the eye. The blind do not see light or colour. Light and colour is only a vibration, which through the eye produce a sensation in our brain which we call light or colour. Thus light and colour are only a vibration, a sensation made manifest through the instrumentality of the physical brain. Brain is not a source. It is only an instrument. The source is the Sun. If the brain—

instrument decays or dies, the cause of sensation viz. the Sun, does not die. It exists because the same cause produces similar sensation on millions of other brain-instruments. This shows that the cause exists independently of the brain and that there is existence beyond the physical world.

During a hypnotic spell, activity of the physical brain is arrested, with the result that memory of forgotten incidents, of incidents of weak vibrations, also gets through. If the mind activity is consciously controlled, if the physical brain is quietened, one can consciously recall memory of all incidents. To recall memory, suitable conditions have to be created and the condition is stillness of physical brain activity. Just as when a cinema picture is projected on a screen placed in strong day light, no picture is visible; but if the day light is decreased, the picture shows itself, and when it is completely dark, the picture is most distinct. Memory of those incidents can be recalled which have been sensed by the brain in the past. A song which has never been heard can never be re-called. A scene that has not been witnessed cannot be remembered. Thus our physical brain will bring through the memory of those incidents that it has experienced. If something happens, while a person is asleep, he can never know what was happening, nor can he ever recall it. Just as a radio-set can transmit sound of those wave lengths to which it is tuned, the brain can transmit memory of only those incidents which had produced impression on it, howsoever weak.

The brain of an individual was born with him. It has never lived before and it dies at his physical death. As such, it cannot bring through the memory of past lives, because it had no part in them. It never has sensed the past lives. The brain has no past.

The past is stored in the invisible store-house, in an invisible consciousness that belongs to the thinker. This consciousness finds expression through the brain and the degree of expression depends upon the refinement of the brain. It can express or transmit all that the thinker sends to it, whether present or past, if the brain is refined to respond to the subtle vibrations of the thinker. If a person can raise his consciousness beyond the brain-consciousness and identify himself with the thinker—consciousness, he can see his whole past, the past that belonged to the brains of his past incarnations.

The human consciousness exists before human conception and after his death. Consciousness is imperishable. It seeks to manifest itself through the agency of the physical brain. It is this consciousness that reincarnates in each succeeding body, everytime endeavouring to have a more and more refined and evolved body so that it can manifest itself in a greater degree.This is evolution of consciousness. Then the past lives can be remembered. Many do. Buddha remembered his past 500 lives. Several others get fragments of their past which explains their present conditions.

HOW DID THE COSMOS COME INTO EXISTENCE

Before we consider reincarnation, it is necessary to know why this world and man were created. What need had God to create? It is a difficult question to answer, because it can be answered only by one who is one with Him and knows His mind. But using the method of inference, by observing what obtains in nature, it may be possible to understand this why.

Everything in the cosmos is moving. Life is dynamic. Nothing is ever stationary. Earth, stars, planets, sun, moon, all are forever moving. Air is never at rest; water is always in motion; fire is always jumping or spreading. All things, the entire creation is made of molecules and atoms. Atoms are made of protons and electrons. Electrons are all the time, going around the protons. Protons and electrons are charges of positive and negative electricity. Electricity itself is vibration, motion. Everything, from the smallest to the largest, is incessant motion. What appears immobile, like a mountain, is going round with the rotating and revolving earth, and every molecule of it is vibrating. Nothing ever is at rest. The fundamental property of all that exists is movement. It, therefore, is safe to conclude that the basic property of the cause of creation - life, God or whatever name we give it - is Motion. Motion implies Energy. Nothing can move without Force and Energy. Therefore, Energy is the fundamental property of God. "In the beginning was the Word, Word was with God. Word was God." Word is sound. Sound is produced by vibration and is propogated by vibration of the medium through which it passes. Through this vibration, this Motion, this Energy, was the Cosmos created. In the beginning was the Word - by uttering the Word, Energy was released; and this Energy was the cause of manifestation. Om is *shabd.* Om is the word. Om is the beginning of creation. Om is God.

All things are made of the five primordial elements: *akash*, air, fire, water and earth. *Shabd* is carried through *akash*. *Shabd* energises *akash. Akash* pervades the whole universe. Vibrating akash, put the whole universe in turmoil, and the universe came to life. The interplay of these akashik vibrations produced grosser matter, air. Air is ever on the move. Energy of the ever-moving air, vibrations of the air, inter-acting, produce fire. Without the heat of friction and by the oxygen supplied by air, there can be no fire. Fire is ever vibrating, jumping, expanding. The interplay of heat vibration produces vapour; and by cold is the vapour condensed to water. Water is always in the state of motion. Inter-action of water produces solid matter - Earth. Leave water in a pond and solid matter, green moss, appears. Earth and its molecules are never at rest. And out of these five elements are the rest of the things produced.

All the molecules that are air, fire, water and earth were thus produced from vibration, from energy, and can be reconverted into energy. Science has proved that matter and energy are interchangeable. Science, therefore, says that one thing from which all is created is energy. Energy, therefore, is the characteristic of the creator, God.

Movement is Life. Stop movement and you produce Death. Confine air in a closed room and in a few hours, it shall have died. It becomes stale. Confine water in a vessel, in a pond, and it stagnates, dies. It cannot be used, it is poisonous. It will produce death. Confine fire to a closed room; it will be suffocated to death extinguished. Let a baby not throw out its arms and legs, it will not grow. Don't move your hand or arm for a considerable time and it will atrophy. Don't let the growing shrubs shake in air, they will not gain strength to withstand storms. Don't let the diaphragm of the stomach move and food will not be digested and assimilated. Don't let the heart pump and life is extinguished. Don't exercise your intellect, and you become a dullard. Don't let the trains and aeroplanes move, and civilization dwindles. Think of anything. It implies movement, and hence life. Stop movement, life stops. Life and movement i.e. energy, go together.

Energy is movement. Movement implies change. It is by movement, by interplay of vibrations, that all created life is produced. Hence change is the Law of Life. Since energy, movement, change come from God as the Prime Cause, Energy and the consequent change are His very nature, and so was the creation created and it must continuously change. But how does change necessitiate reincarnation?

DESIRE TO CHANGE NECESSITATES INVOLUTION AND EVOLUTION

Everything that starts from a source, goes outwards to the farthest limits and then again comes back to the source. Throw a stone in a pond of water. Waves start from the point where the stone fall. They go forth outwards to the boundry of the pond and return to the point from where they started. Water originally comes from the ocean, and wherever it is, whether in clouds or mountains or rivers or land, it tends to flow back to the ocean. All fire first comes from the Sun, and wherever it is, it tends upwards towards the Sun. We start from home everyday, and after the day's work tend to come back home. Going forth is involution; coming back is evolution. Going forth is descending from the subtlest to the grossest and coming back is ascending from the grossest to the subtlest. This two-way business involves continuous change and change means newer and newer forms, necessitating transformation and reincarnation of the original essence.

This fundamental quality to change, to go forth and return is accomplished by involution and evolution. And all that is, is only a part of this process., Whatever one sees or whatever exists is there because it is fulfilling this urge of accomplishing this process.

HOW CAN SUBTLE ESSENCE FORM GROSS MATTER

We cannot see God we cannot feel Him. We cannot know anything about Him. He is so subtle. How can then such subtle essence produce the gross matter? How can Akash produce grosser matter from air to earth?

All cosmos is made of one primordial substance. This substance by differentiation becomes millions of different things we come across. That such a differentiation exists and is possible is amply exhibited and established by science, e.g. force is a subtle thing; it, acting as a chemical force, brings two subtle matters H_2, O_2 together and forms grosser matter, water. Action and reaction of a very subtle thing on two other subtle thing produce gross matter. Again, action of a subtle element, heat, (by extracting heat) converts water into ice, a much grosser material, and by applying heat to water a grosser matter can be converted into vapour - a subtle matter. Water cannot be formed without H_2 and O_2. Thus the existence of a gross matter depends upon bringing two subtle matters together. Take away the subtle components and water ceases to be. Conversely, gross matter, ice, by play of heat force, can be converted into more refined matter, water and steam. Or by passing a much subtler force viz. electricity through water, it can be split up into subtler material, H_2 and O_2.

Subtle force like gravity produces physical results: one can fall and break one's neck or leg or arm; a roof can collapse and destroy man and material; earth, moon and other planets move because of this force and produce day and night, seasons, and a lot more of very material phenomena. A much subtler force like electricity acting on gross matter produces light, heat, coolness; it can run machinery and trains; it can destroy life.

Science has shown that all matter is made of electricity. Everything consists of atoms. Atoms are made of protons and electrons, positive and negative charges of electricity. Atom of one element differs from the atom of another element, only in the difference of number of electrons contained in them. Take away one or more electrons from an atom, and it becomes quite a different substance. Thus differentiation of electric charge produces atoms of different elements. Changes in the subtle components of compounds bring about changes in its physical or grosser form, transforming one matter into another. This is differentiation from subtlest to grossest. We cannot see electricity, atoms, molecules, but we can see their result - matter. Subtle force, when it becomes objectified, becomes matter, gross force. Matter is gross and energy subtle, yet they are interchangeable.

Interaction of subtler force and gross matter creates more and different forms. Vegetation absorbs minerals and other substances it needs from earth, nitrogen and carbondioxide from the atmosphere to build its physical form, but it can grow only in the presence of solar energy. Deny it this subtle force and it will decay. It is only in the presence of light, a subtle matter, that a photograph can be taken. Minerals produce vegetation, vegetation produces animal and human world and from human it goes on to the Divine. The gross food we eat is converted into blood, energy and nerve force which are subtler. Thus subtle to gross and gross to subtle are the processes we are surrounded by. Infact life is life on account of this two-way process.

This, therefore, seems to be the process by which the manifested world has been created viz. differentiation of the subtlest matter into the grossest—involution; and again re-transformation of the grossest into the subtlest—evolution. The primordial substance at its rarest or subtlest is spirit and at its grossest is physical matter. All things in between contain spirit and matter in different degrees.

Science divides matter into three states—solid, liquid and gas. In each of these states, there is a large number of varied things. Similarly, cosmic matter is divided in seven well-defined states or planes. On each plane is a great degree of variation. These states or planes do not exist in different spaces, but co-exist, inter-penetrating one another, just as lights from a number of lamps in a room co-exist, penetrating one another, or just as sand, water, air and other can co-exist in a bottle; or just as a solute co-exists in a solvent without occupying extra space.

The three states of matter of science are occasioned by the difference of force of attraction associated with the molecules. So are the planes different in character on account of the different degree of consciousness (Spirit) exhibiting itself on different planes. In fact, these planes may be considered as seven planes of consciousness, from pure consciousness to negligible amount of consciousness, operating through the grossest physical matter.

Now, in order to differentiate matter, or in order to create different forms, or in order to transform them, and in order to maintain continuous change, force or energy is required. According to science, all world is made of matter and energy, matter and energy, both are inter-changeable. Similarly, for the seven states of cosmic matter, for differentiating, for evolution, a force is needed. This force is the Universal mind, the *Manesputra*, the thinker in man. This force, the mind, comes from the fifth plane, the mind itself being the fifth principle. This mind or thought is the force that creates and fashions the different forms we see. As in cosmos, so in the man, this fifth principle, the thinker, fashions his form and evolution. It is the guiding force at the back of all that man is and can become.

That thought, the subtle matter, can create form is proved by hypnoticism. Again, thought has effect on the formation of our physiognomy and on the expression of our face. A noble thought can transform an ugly face into a divine one, and a vicious thought can transform a beautiful face into an ugly one.

Blades of a rotating table fan, rotating fast, become a solid disc. They will not allow anything to pass through them. Fighting with stick was well known in ancient India. One man, rotating one stick would keep a crowd away from him. Thin threads, forming warp and weft produce a non-transparent cloth. The solidity of substances depends upon the nature of their atoms. Atoms derive their nature from the intricate patterns produced by the rotation and vibration of the electrons in them. Thus there is ample proof that subtle matter can produce dense form and dense matter can become subtle. Action of subtle matter on matter of different degrees of grossness produces different phenomena. The huge lot of phenomena is due to a large variety of permutations and combinations of inter-action of spirit and matter. Having produced gross matter through which it can hardly exhibit itself, the spirit sets itself the task of refining it, so that it can exhibit itself more and more till it can exhibit itself perfectly.

Instances to corrobarate this possibility are not wanting. Light, a subtle substance, acting on gross particles in atmosphere, produces beautiful phenomena of the blue of the sky; red and other hues at sunrise and sunset. Light falling on drops of water produces rainbow. Light passing through prism produces different colours. Colours, rainbow and sky do not exist. Look at a lamp through your kerchief, and you find beautiful geometric patterns formed. Look at light through half closed eyes and you witness beautiful phenomena.

Light falling on a brick cannot get through it. The brick is too gross, too dense to respond to the vibrations of light. Yet, it is possible to refine the earth in the brick so as to become transparent. Glass is made from silica (earth). Again, glass in the form of a lens in a vehicle through which light produces a huge lot of phenomena—spectacles, telescopes, mircroscopes, glazed windows. Glass is in the form of a mirror becomes vehicle for light for quite a different kind of phenomenon.

INVOLUTION AND EVOLUTION IN PHYSICAL WORLD

Science accepts evolution. The process depends upon two principles: the tendency to vary and the tendency of the environment to influence the variation, either favourably or unfavourably. Thus the germ of life that wants to vary selects suitable environments for its growth. But if it cannot select suitable conditions or comes across unsuitable environments, it either adapts itself to the environments or if it does not adjust, dies. This leads to the idea of natural selection and the struggle for existence. Weaker goes to the wall. This evolution continuous from mineral kingdom, through vegetable and animal kingdoms, to the human kingdom.

Change of form is necessary for evolution. Hence, Nature breaks up mineral form to create vegetable form. Vegetable form is eaten up i.e. destroyed, to produce animal form and animal life is sacrificed to develop human form. In each category of form, one destroys the other. Animals destroy vegetation; one animal kills the other, one man destroys the other so that he may live. Nature does not preserve forms. On the dead body of one form, it builds another. Nature is interested in evolution and not in preserving form. Death is the process by which nature achieves evolution of form, to make it ready for other principles, to act and react on it to again produce something new.

Thus nature is red in tooth and claw. There is death all around. But nature, in this process, is every moment pushing ahead evolution. It is creating newer and better forms, destroying weaker and primitive forms. The death is of the form and not of life. All through this process. Life is exhibiting itself. Destruction is there, because life asserts itself. The higher form is created by sacrifice of the lower form.

Science has shown that the earth and the universe were created millions of years ago and that it has reached the present stage after passing through innumerable changes. All things have gradually been changing from simpler to complex patterns. Our earth was a nebulous mass, consisting of gases. It has gradually cooled down, through aeons, to the present solid form, and is still changing. So is the case with other heavenly bodies. Through the same process of change, of differentiation, of evolution, did life, starting with minute germs of life, become plants, insects, fishes, reptiles, birds, animals and men. Man was produced much after planets and animals came into existence. It took billions of years for him to evolve out of animals, loss his tail, learn to stand erect, work with his fingers, and speak, and again millions of years for the first primitive animal-man to become man as he is today. Man is the epitome of the whole creation. The embryo, after conception, passes through the gamut of evolution, from polyp, fish, reptile, dog and ape, before it becomes a human babe. Science has shown how a higher animal form has been evolved from a lower one. Evolution has been from simpler to complex, till the stage of man has been reached. Hindu philosophy also accepts the principle of evolution. Kapila explained evolution scientifically in the seventh century B.C., long before the Christian era, and long before the present science came to the same conclusion.

In this evolutionary process, progress is preserved by passing it on from one generation to the next. The peculiarities of behaviour created by force of circumstances i.e. by adaptation are transmitted. Whenever environments effect change in the organs of an organism, the physical changes and adaptations are transmitted. Camel is an animal of the desert. In desert, water is not found easily. It is necessary to store water. Camel developed organs and method of storing water. This is transmitted. Again, desert is all sand. It would be difficult to walk with small hoofs like those of a cow or a deer or a lion. Camel developed large, flat feet, so that it could walk easily on sand. This is transmitted. Transmission of the original or adapted characteristics is called Heredity. Peculiarities of physiognomy or organic defects resulting in diseases are transmitted. Toothlessness, constipation, tendency to greying of hair and several other traits are transmitted by Heredity. But Heredity transmits physical traits only.

Law of Heredity, thus, means the tendency of the parents to transmit the peculiarities of their own organism to their offspring e.g. a horse will produce a horse; lion a lion; man a man. Peculiar differences in the same species are also transmitted. Thats' why a European, an Indian, an African, a chinese can be recognised and distinguished. Thus there is a physical unity or similarity, and it is transmitted in such a striking degree that an offspring of a particular species will be always and easily recognised as belonging to that species. A dog cannot be mistaken for a goat; a lion cannot be mistaken for a horse; a man cannot be mistaken for a monkey. While the difference of characteristics between the different species is considerable enough to distinguish one from the other, the difference of characteristics between the individuals of the same species are confined to a narrow range. A horse from whatever part of the world and with whatever differences will always be recognised as a horse. A human being from whatever race and whatever place will be recognised as a human being.

But the moral and intellectual differences present a different picture. While in animals of the same species, moral and intellectual differences vary, but slightly, differences in the human species vary through a very long range. While one race can count only up to ten, another can conceive of numbers going into billions and billions. In one race treachery and head-hunting is a credit; in another honesty and self-sacrifice is honoured. Thus, it is only in the human form that we find physical unity, but tremendous moral and mental divergence.

Life of animals of any species, say, cow deer or ants, has always been the same throughout the ages. Their methods, their behaviour, their instincts, their social life, their over-all pattern of life have remained the same, age after age. There has been no evolution on the moral and intellectual side. Whereas, man started his career as an animal, but there has been a tremendous change, evolution of moral and mental qualities. What has wrought this difference? While animal has remained stationary, man has progressed vastly. There should, therefore, be some other force that looks to the moral and mental evolution. And this force must be different from the force that brings about physical evolution, because if it were the same force, its moral and mental potentialities would have been exhibited in the animal world also.

It is recognised principle in nature that all that exists in the seed can become manifest in the fruit; but fruit cannot have qualities that were not latent in the seed. *Vedanta* also draws attention to this principle when it says. "There is nothing in the end which was also not in the beginning." That is, there can be no manifestation of that which was not latent. Man also, having evolved from the lowest animal life can only have qualities latent in the seed i.e. we can only have animal qualities or animal nature—e.g. animal prospensities, sense enjoyments, self-preservation, fear of death, etc.

But man has another set of qualities which do not exist in animals - truthfulness, control of senses, self-sacrifice, helpfulness, compassion, forgiveness, devotion etc. These qualities would have been suicidal to the growth of the animal qualities. They, in fact, would be a curb on the evolutionary process. As such these qualities could not have been derived through the evolutionary process as observed by science.

SPIRIT REINCARNATING PRINCIPLE

Thus the law of heredity can only explain the transmission of physical characteristics and the theory of evolution can explain only the evolution of the physical form. And yet man, humanity, does evolve, have been evolving, spiritually through the ages. Therefore, it is reasonable to suppose that there necessarily is some moral and intellectual or spiritual force which acting on man produces spiritual evolution. And not only that, it has to be accepted that there is some element, some principle, which persists through man, which, though not subject to the law of heredity, goes on evolving and exhibiting its evolution through the physical man. The only possible explanation of this can be that there is a principle that is permanent, which gathers experience and evolves, is separate and distinct from the animal-man, inhabits the human form during its span of life, separates at the death of the human form; again inhabits a new human form and further evolves, and will continue till the moral, mental and spiritual qualities have been perfected. Then will the purpose of creation be fulfilled and the created reach the creator. It is this permanent principle which reincarnates in the human body. The complete explanation can, thus, be found in the animal or material evolution till it reaches its perfection in the human form and thence forward the evolution of the spirit through reincarnation. The two combined yield the complete explanation of the process and purpose of life.

The above explanation looks more plausible since it satisfactorily explains problems like:

1. Heredity cannot transmit spiritual qualities, because the spiritual qualities do not belong to the material aspect of life but to consciousness or the incarnating ego.

2. Animals or the lowest human races do not respond to even the most elementary moral conception, but the advanced races accept them readily. This is because in the advanced races exists the evolved reincarnating ego.

3. In members of a family, family likeness can be seen because it is transmitted. But in the same family, there is a great divergence in the moral and intellectual qualities of the members. This divergence is due to their being different egos, with different degrees of evolution in them. Two twins may be physically exactly alike, and yet when they grow up their characters are often diametrically opposite.

4. There are cases on record when small children have shown genius in arts, music, mathematics etc. They were not trained and yet their mastery over the subject is stupendously greater than of those who have spent long years in taking training. Nor have their parents been geniuses so that the genius has been transmitted. And if genius could be transmitted, why should it be transmitted only to one child, and why not to others also? But usually genius is born of mediocre parents. Mozart, Plato, Bruno, Newton, Shakespeare, Einstein, Patanjali, Kalidas, Yajanavalkya etc. are cases in point. Birth of Rama, Krishna, Buddha, Christ etc. cannot be explained by the principle of heredity. Whence came their brilliance?

5. Two equally clever persons are presented with an explanation of philosophic, ethical or scientific problem. One understands easily; the other does not get it at all. It only means that one has known it before and for him it is only revision, but to the other it is something quite new and it takes time to grasp a new thing.

6. Race evolution would also point towards the existence of a reincarnating ego. If life was one single existence, there would be no evolution of the race. There would be evolution of the individual during the span of his life from birth to death and then the end. But if race evolution is a fact, then it postulates the existence of what is *Soul* which evolves while reincarnating. Experiences gained are accumulated by the invisible *Soul* and not by the physical body. The *Soul* is indestructible and precisely because it is eternal, it can evolve.

EXPLANATION OF 'TENDENCY TO VARY'

One of the fundamental basis of evolution theory is 'tendency to vary'. But science does not, because it cannot, explain the source of this tendency to vary; nor does science talk of the laws that control and guide the tendency to vary. The answer is, however, given by the doctrine of reincarnations.

Vedanta and science say that 'There is nothing in the end which was not also in the beginning." This law governs the process of evolution as well as the law of causation. The desire of the potential to become manifest, conditioned by environments, causes variation. When matter and spirit both begin to evolve, action and reaction creates infinite varieties. In human form, the varieties are manifested in human individuals being of different capacities. With growth certain latent powers grow and those that are strongest manifest, overcoming others that are weaker, and overcoming any environmental obstructions. The weaker ones await suitable environment for manifesting themselves and gain strength. This desire causes variation.

Having come to the conclusion that there is some spiritual principle which is eternal, permanent, that it is this principle that evolves by reincarnating in the human bodies, that this principle is different from the one that evolved through material range - mineral to human form - it is worthwhile considering what constitutes the whole gamut of evolution—material and spiritual.

PURPOSE AND URGE FOR REINCARNATION

The very nature of the Creator, the original cause, the spirit, is energy, vibration, change, expansion and contraction, and so life goes forth - involution, and must come back - evolution. This evolution part is accomplished through reincarnation. Thus, the purpose of reincarnation is to evolve or grow through experience and to know the ultimate truth. Desire for knowledge is the urge. The individual souls or thinkers are seeds of the universal soul and like the seeds of a tree, contain the same potentialities as the universal soul. But again like the seeds of a tree, the souls must grow by unfoldment, by experience, by knowledge, before they too become the tree or merge into the universal soul.

The seed, in order to grow and manifest must go deep down into earth, the gross matter, absorb minerals, water and gases in presence of solar energy, so as the soul goes deep down into gross physical body, act, learn, experience and evolve. It is this desire of the ego to know, to grow, to unfold its potential qualities that is the force behind reincarnation. It is this desire that makes the ego descend into the physical form, time after time, till it has completely unfolded itself.

But why should consciousness or ego condition itself by gross matter? Why can it not evolve without gross matter?

Pure consciousness, by pronouncing the word, and by continuous differentiation, produced grosser and grosser matter till the grossest matter, earth or minerals was formed. Atma, the first principle, by differentiation, produced other principles, seven in number. All principles came from the same source and must again move to the same source, like the waves in a pond. Each principle evolves separately, then acts on other principles, and reacting evolves, so that all the seven principles move together as one single whole to reunite with the origin, just as the white light breaks up into seven colours and it is again the re-combination of all the seven colours that can produce white light.

Again, by its very inherent nature, though pure consciousness can produce grosser matter by differentiation, it cannot penetrate through gross matter, just as light cannot penetrate through a slab of stone, but it can through a slab of glass (Which is matter refined for the purpose of light). The matter has to be refined so that the consciousness may work through it and exhibit itself.

After the physical death, when the link between the body and the consciousness is broken, consciousness is active on the astral plane. Then astral stock-taking takes place. One suffers on account of the non-fulfilment of undesirable habits learnt on the physical plane and consolidates the good astral qualities. This period constitutes the so called 'purgatory'. After completion of this work, link with astral body is also snapped and the astral body dies. Consciousness then acts on the mental plane where stock-taking of mental qualities takes place, eradicating the undesirable traits and strengthening the desirable ones. This period constitutes 'Heaven'. Here 'character' is formed for the next incarnation. One stays a much longer time on this plane.

On the astral and the mental planes, one is in contact with those whom one admires and loves. The contact is astral and mental. One learns by contact as much as one does on earth. Infact, the contacts are much easier and intenser on account of easier movement unhampered by the denser physical body. On these planes, life goes on in much the same way as on earth! only it is more intense. Sufferings and joys are more acute on account of the greater sensitiveness of the astral and mental matter. Hence, sufferings constitute hell and joys constitute heaven.

Later on, the mental body is also discarded; it dies; and only pure consciousness, *Manasputra,* remains. *Manasputra* in light of this experience of the present incarnation as also of the previous incarnations, then plans and decides what shall be the form of the next body, and in accordance with that are the new causal, astral and physical bodies prepared for the next incarnation.

The new body built is in conformity with the sum total of experience accumulated or 'Character' formed. Every desire existing in the character has to be fulfilled. The new body to be built will be such that its sense organs are capable of expressing some of the intense desires in their corresponding intensities.

This would explain the phenomena of born geniuses or that one is good from his birth and the other vicious. This would also explain what Christ said about the man born blind. Even in the same incarnation effect of thought can be seen in new likes and dislikes and changes produced in temperament and ideas and character. Thus the physical, astral and mental bodies are only for one incarnation. For every new incarnation, they are different and new. It is the Manasputra that is eternal.

After one has exhausted the experiences of his previous incarnation, consolidated all that had to be consolidated and eliminated all that needed elimination; and after sufficient rest, he desires for more experience. This desire is inherent in the Manas, just as stomach desires more food after it has digested the previous one; or when one has acquired a piece of knowledge, after assimilating it, he desires for more. The consciousness gets ready for the next plunge in the physical matter. The moment this desire for more knowledge and experience arises, the consciousness attracts round it mental and astral matter out of which is fashioned the mental and astral bodies. These bodies go on working on their own planes, sharpening the faculties through which experience is sought during the next incarnation. At this stage the masters of Karma with unerring justice and unerring knowledge, guide the astral body to the place and to the parents and to the environments most suited to the progress and to working out of karma. The etheric double is filled in with grosser physical matter, conception takes place and the consciousness is linked to the foetus. A new life, a new schooling, a new period of experience commences.

For the first two or three years the mental, the astral and the physical bodies—the instruments of the consciousness—are in the formative stage. The consciousness has to continually act on them to make them respond to its tune. During this period of formation, the effect of education from parents is tremendous.

When the Manas ensouls a human body, the body is not yet dense enough or gross enough. Hence it acts on the astral matter of the body producing pyschic phenomena like clairvoyance, clairaudience, telepathy, intuition, etc. Animals have these powers as also babies. But as the body grows and becomes denser, the vibrations of the Manas have now to move heavier matter and the effect is slowed down. Action on this heavier matter produces intellectual qualities like logic, reasoning, rationalism, etc. These are the processes of the brain - mind, slow and deliberative and need the elaboration of language. When intellect gets perfected, the brain is trained to respond directly to the subtler vibrations of the Manas and so have psychic perceptions. The difference between these psychic and the earlier psychic perception is that while the earlier perception worked unconsciously, the animal - brain not being conscious of them, the latter and used consciously by the brain. Man becomes the master of these perceptions or powers and uses them as his tools as he uses his tongue or his reasoning as his conscious tools. Thus, the psychic powers are combined with intellectual experience.

At present humanity has reached high intellectual level and is moving towards acquiring the psychic powers consciously. Masters are persons who have achieved this.

After this evolution is completed on earth, there are different evolutions on other spheres. The perfected one, the enlightened one, the Arhat, chooses his next path or stays on, like Buddha, to serve humanity, to help humanity evolve and mature. This is the great Renunciation.

Body of alternating sexes is provided to bland the qualities peculiar to both and so create a perfect being.

The interval between two incarnations depends upon the length of the preceding life; on the intensity of the preceding earth life; on level of development. Period varies from a few years to 1500 years; average being 500 years.

EXPLANATION OF WHY THERE IS NO PAST MEMORY

Now it will be easy to see why man does not remembers his past. The ego is surrounded by mental, astral and physical bodies. While the mental body is transparent, the causal body, carrying emotions, desires and feelings, is so criss-cross that it is difficult to see through it; and the physical is so dense as to prevent the Mansic vibrations to pass through. Hence a man cannot see inwards and even if he tries to, gets a distorted view of the ego and hence what he sees is not reliable. But it is possible for a human being to evolve and control these bodies and see through them i.e. he can teach his bodies to respond to the vibrations of the Manas, and then he can recall his whole past. In an average man the physical brain is never still, it is always responding to the external vibrations of the Manas. If the vibrations of the physical brain are controlled and the brain made receptive, vibrations of the Manas could be perceived.

But the memory is not altogether absent. During the present and the past reincarnations, the reincarnating ego has taken decision as to what is right and what is wrong. The experience has pointed out what is right and what is wrong and this is conveyed to the brain—consciousness by the 'Voice of Conscience'. Conscience is the memory of the past decisions.

There are cases on record of these who have direct knowledge and know their past. Some children remember their previous life and have recognised their parents and house, etc.

On the doctrine of reincarnation it would be easy to explain a number of problems that ordinarily boffle the human mind.

The apparent differences of intellect, character, position, status, richness etc. that look unjust and whimsical can now be understood. The reincarnating ego has fashioned the body and a person is placed in environments calculated to help his education and evolution. Things of earth are meant to give experience and knowledge. They, by themselves, have no value. They are temporary and perishable things and are used as mere tools; and these tools are chosen by the reincarnating ego himself. Conditions are not imposed from outside. Thus there is no whim, no injustice. The differences are due to different stages of knowledge and experiences gained; differences are due to difference in the age of the reincarnating ego. When all egos have reached the end, there will be no differences between them, just as all those who graduate from a university have equal status though some graduate at one time and others at a later date.

Reincarnations explains the problem of evil and good. There is no such thing as evil. In a man, animal, appetites appear as evil. As he evolves and learns to universalise these desires and sublimate them into divine qualities, it appears as good in him. Evil, thus, is unawakened state. It is a problem in time and not a problem in morality.

In a given set of environments different persons react differently and evolve differently. This is due to the difference in their egos. Each ego reacts according to his experience and his requirements. Just as different seeds sown in the same land under similar conditions, draw different substances and in different quantities from the same environment and grow differently. In the same garden grow apples and oranges and mangoes—all are different things growing in the same environment. The difference is in the potentialities in the seed. Similarly, the difference in human beings is due to difference in the latent desires which want to manifest themselves. Our desires and thoughts do not get destroyed. Nothing is destroyed. Our desires and thoughts remain latent when we die, and want to manifest themselves during the next reincarnation.

Reincarnation explains death. Life is dynamic, never the same at any two moments. Everything is continuously changing. Change means that what existed before has disappeared or died and something new has taken its place or something has been born. The same thing has been born in a new form. There is continuous death and continuous rebirth. What really happens is *Change*, but we express it as death and birth, and as birth and death. This idea is embodied in what Krishna said to Arjuna:

"Certain is death for the born; certain is birth for the dead;

over that which is enevitable thou shouldst not grieve."

Our physical body could not grow and live unless it died, every moment. Death is condition and sign of life.

Consciousness progresses by riding on matter. Continuous change or death of matter gives the consciousness the opportunity to experience and progress. It is the form that is ever dying; Life continuous.

Thus, if we realise that life in this world is a school to gain experience and knowledge, where hardships and difficulties mean intense education and greater opportunity for progress while easy life will mean slow education and less opportunities for growth, life will have a different meaning, and we can appreciate life in its proper perspective. We shall not be depressed by pain and misery, we shall put forth a greater effort and shall enjoy the struggle of conquering the animal nature in us.

17

Can We Communicate With God?

The word 'God' in the question, "Can We Communicate With God" includes God, gods, goddesses, rishis, munis and the advanced souls who are beyond the physical plane. We can speak to God and He responds. Not only that, He watches over us and guides and helps us without our asking.

Man has a limited vision. He can see light within a limited range. He sees light coming from the sun, from red to violet. But there is light beyond the red and beyond the violet—infra-red, ultra-violet, x-rays and many more. The range of vision of all living beings is not the same. For example, man cannot see clearly at night while animals of the forest can. Their range of vision is different from that of man. The existence of light beyond the visible range can be known by scientific instruments. Infra-red, ultra-violet, x-rays etc. can be caught by appropriate photographic plates. Man cannot see atoms, electrons and protons, but they can be caught by photographic films and their existence can be seen by the effects they produce. Light of different kinds varies in its frequency and wave-length. Frequency of red light is less than that of the violet; wave-length of red light is longer than that of the violet light.

Human ear also has limited audition. The range of audition for human ear is vibrations between 33-33,000 per second. Frequency below 33 and above 33,000 cannot be heard by human ear. Frequency higher than 33,000 i.e., above the upper limit of human audition, is called supersonic. All bodies that is vibrate produce sound; every sounding body is vibrating. There are birds who utter notes which are supersonic i.e. of higher frequency than 33,000, but their notes can be recorded by instruments. The earth is whirling through space and produces sound, but human ear cannot record it.

Sound produced while talking involves the use of vocal cords, palate, tongue and lips. But we say that sound is produced by mouth. While speaking, vibrations produced by the mouth are carried to the listener's ear, which vibrates the tympanum. The tympanum sends these vibrations to the brain and are converted by the brain into sound. We talk into the mouth piece of a telephone. The vibrations there are carried by electricity through the wire to the diaphragm in the receiver and make it vibrate. The receiver then sends these vibrations to the tympanum which are converted into sound.

Existence is on physical plane, astral plane and other higher planes. Each higher plane is subtler than its lower plane. Each plane has its own range of vision and audition. The higher the plane, the greater the frequency obtaining there, with the result that there is no inter-communication between these planes and, therefore, man cannot see or hear what exists on other planes. If, however, the frequencies of one plane could be lowered or raised to other planes, inter-communication would become possible. Electric power issuing from the generator in the central power station is of a higher voltage. It is, by means of transformer, lowered to the voltage suitable to the electric appliances used. If not done, the appliances will burn out.

Scientists and medical people who are exercised over this problem of inter-communication between the physical and the higher planes are endeavouring to find ways and means of transforming the frequencies obtaining there to those obtaining on the earth, also those who want to establish contact with the higher planes are experimenting to catch the transformed vibrations. Quite a good amount of work in this direction is being done in the US and USSR as also in some other European countries. Communications, though not satisfactory, have been received by the earth scientists from the higher planes and it would not be surprising if in the next 30 or 40 years, a good communication is established.

At a radio station, programmes are transmitted on different frequencies and each one goes out without interfering with the other. On a receiving set, a programme is obtained by tuning to a particular frequency. If we want a different programme, we have to change the tuning to that frequency. Tuning to one frequency will not get programmes of other frequencies. God is omni-present, omni-scient and omni-potent. He can communicate on any frequency suitable to the occasion. Man, in order to receive his communication, should be able to tune himself to different frequencies. But as it is, man's capacity is limited. His sense of hearing and vision is limited. Then, how can he receive communication from God on frequencies different from what he is capable of? Happily, man has latent power to develop and can, by training, develop to respond to different frequencies. This training comes by spiritual discipline under the guidance of a competent Guru. It does not mean that he who cannot or does not undergo the spiritual discipline cannot communicate with God. Man can be illiterate, uneducated or educated. Intellectual with different IQs. God will respond to everyone of them when called upon. Therefore, He responds by different ways suitable to the person concerned.

When communication is done by word of mouth, the vibration of the speaker's lips reaches the listener's tympanum and is carried to the brain where it is converted into knowledge or consciousness. Language is a series of symbols and the knowledge or consciousness of the brain is produced by this symbol. For example, *apple, seb, suf,* mean the same object, but it has different symbol in different languages. A person used to the symbol "apple" will not understand the symbols "seb" or "suf". Similarly, a person used to the symbol "seb" will not understand the symbols "apple" or "suf". Communication can be established by vision. Eyes can show anger, appreciation, love etc. Touch also can communicate anger, love, appreciation (pat on the back), as also the knowledge of cold and hot. Similarly, knowledge of good and bad comes through smell. Animals, when given something to eat first smell it and find out if it is good for them. Then they eat it or discard it. Taste also conveys knowledge. Thus, knowledge accrues not only from word of mouth but from the exercise of all our senses. Knowledge is conveyed by facial expression, signs and symbols and by touch between man and man. Facial expression of pleasure or displeasure conveys its meaning to the viewer. Intonation in the tone of one's voice carries the speaker's mind to the listener. Touch, by its difference in pressure, hardness, softness, by a pat, conveys knowledge, but facial expression or voice or touch are again dependent on the basic senses of vision, audition and touch. Hence, all methods of communication can be put down to the knowledge comprehended by senses.

God responds to the supplication in the language or in the form which the supplicant can understand. He may appear in a physical form or communicate by inner voice, *akashwani*, dream, signs, symbols, auguries and so forth. While man can communicate with God by prayer, God can communicate in a variety of ways. God, not only responds to our call but may, on his own, give man a warning or guidance.

A few cases may illustrate how God's guidance comes.

1. God appeared as Narasingh Awatara and Gaj Awatara instantly in reply to the supplicants.

2. I came across a book "Idyl of the White Lotus" by Mebel Collins. It was an occult story. I was much impressed. I finished the book the same day. I was so taken up that every day I would borrow a book and complete it. This went on for a month, I was caught up with the idea how to know the "absolute truth" which means God. Then I had a dream:

> "My father, my younger brother and I went out for an after-dinner stroll. A little distance away from our house on a hill side, we saw a *shamiana* and in the centre of that *shamiana* was a smaller *shamiana* from which seven brilliant lights could be seen. On enquiry, we found that seven masters had come down and anybody could meet them. There was a ticket of Rs. 3 for the outer *shamiana* and Rs. 5 for the inner *shamiana* where the Masters were seated. I was very much keen because here was a chance to meet the Master K.H. (His full name is Koot Hoomi) and enquire from him how to know the absolute truth. I told my father and brother to go in first, meet the Master, enquire from Him how to know the absolute truth and then I will go and meet Him after they return. My father and brother went in and when they came out, I caught hold of my father by both arms and, enquired what did the Master say about knowing the absolute truth. I was so much excited that I woke up. And as I was waking up, came a voice from the void `Akashwani' saying. "By self-sacrifice, I felt sorry for waking up and missing the chance to meet the Master."

But I was happy that I got a reply to my query. Evidently, I was not yet considered fit enough to have the Master's *darshan*. This was the reply by Akashwani to my query. The word 'self-sacrifice' was loaded with so vast and deep a meaning that since 1923, I have been still discovering its meaning.

3. I was a Professor in Karachi College and often used to be appointed as an examiner to the University of Bombay. Once I received a telegram asking me to proceed immediately to Bombay to conduct the B.Sc. practical examination two days later. In those days, reaching Bombay from Karachi meant changing four trains. From Karachi to Hyderabad (Sind), from Hyderabad(Sind) to Marwar, from Marwar to Ahmedabad and from Ahmedabad to Bombay. I had a first class ticket and there was no problem in finding a berth from Karachi to Ahmedabad. But from Ahmedabad to Bombay was a difficult problem. The train went over-crowded. I had no reservation and I knew it would not be easy to find a seat in Ahmedabad-Bombay train. A few minutes before reaching Ahmedabad, I prayed for help for a seat in the train so that I could reach Bombay the next morning and conduct the examination. If I did not reach in time, there was naturally to be some trouble. I was assured thus: "I was told that Ahmedabad-Bombay train was standing at Ahmedabad platform. In front of a compartment stood a man in white dress. A few steps away stood a vendor." This meant that I would find a seat in that compartment.

As I arrived at Ahmedabad station, I hurried to the waiting train. In the hurry and anxiety, I forgot all about the scene I had seen. I moved along the waiting train to find a seat. First class coaches were full and the passengers inside would not open the door. Similar was the condition of the second class. I tried to get into a third class compartment, but third-class compartments were over-crowded and to enter them was impossible. I was worried and moved along the length of the train in search of a seat. I came to a four-berth third class coupe and looking in found that only two berths were occupied. In those days, a four-berth third class coupe was attached to the first class compartment for the attendants of first class passengers. Standing at the door was an attendant in white dress, I asked him if I could get in. He said, "Oh yes, do come in", and grabbed by luggage from the collie then be spread my bed on the upper berth and asked me to go to sleep and that he would wake me up in the morning at Bombay. I changed into my casuals and as I was lying down, I remembered the scene and realised that this is what I was shown.

4. Sitting in meditation, an old mendicant appeared, bent, leaning on a staff naked except for a lion cloth. He said, "trouble is coming to you." "What shall I do to prevent it?" "Give Rs. 3 in charity." "Why shall I give it to you?" He smiled and said,"do not give it to me, give it into Guru langar" Later, I found that Guru Nanak's birthday was three days hence and langar was organised on that day.

5. My father was posted at Quetta. His family was not with him. He was alone. He used to get up early in the morning at 5 a.m., heat up water for his bath and attend to his routine before going to office. One day, he did not feel like getting up from his bed. Then he saw the door of his room open and a boy servant appearing there. He said, "Babuji, water for bath is ready." Father got up with a start wondering what it could be. He had no servant. This was his Master helping him.

6. I did not want to marry. I had planned my life in my own way. I had a large circle of friends. Several girls had proposed to me, but I made them understand that I was not marrying at all. There was a little schooling girl, ten-eleven years old, of whom I was very fond. As time went on, she got very much attached to me and our love grew. Our whole circle knew of this love. She had no mother and no sister. I was her friend, philosopher and guide. She grew up, took a Master's degree and became Principal of a school. I was a Professor of Physics and was going to Bombay to do some research work. I went to see her and say good-bye to her. I told her that now she had grown up, had a fine job, it was time she got married. She replied, "Marry! How can I marry anybody after having known you." I stood spell-bound. How did ever the thought of marrying me enter her? During the fifteen years of our friendship, I had not so much as even embraced her. My love for her was entirely fraternal. I soon left and was very greatly disturbed. What was I to do? On the one hand was my planned bachelor life; on the other was the question that if I did not marry her, she might feel frustrated and her life might become miserable. I went home and from 12 noon to 6 p.m., I was pacing my room debating this question. When my servant announced dinner, I brushed him aside. Six hours of intense thinking and arguing brought to me no solution. Mentally and physically exhausted, I laid down on the carpet on the floor and saw that I was standing on a sea-shore. There were high winds and high waves. To my left, I saw a white launch approaching. I wondered who these fool-hardy people could be to venture out on the sea in such a rough weather. The launch approached, and stopped in front of me. Sea-shore is not like the bank of a river. So the launch was about twenty meters away from me. On one side of the launch was sitting my master and on the benches of the launch were sitting a number of girls. I could not recognise anyone. A girl, in white, sat in the middle. I could not see her face. It was blanked out. Though I was not shown her face, her figure was not that of my friend. The meaning was clear, namely, if I have to marry, I will marry this girl, a different one. My mind got settled and I left for Bombay, the next day.

A few years later as I sat with my Guru, he asked me what I was doing. I replied that I was wasting my time, my father was dead, my brothers and sisters were all well-settled and nobody needed my help. He said, "Then, why not renounce the world." "Right now, Sir," I said. He thought for a few moments and said. "We shall see tomorrow morning." When I met him the next morning, he looked into my eyes and said, "Go and get married." I was stunned. He knew that I did not want to marry. He knew all about me. He noticed my face growing pale and bewilderment in my eyes. He shook his head and said, "Karmic responsibility has to be settling fulfilled." I folded my hands and said, "One request, Sir". "Yes?" "No children." "Accepted." I took up a postcard from his table and wrote to my mother that I was prepared to marry and that she should accept the first offer.

A week later, when I went home, mother told me that I was betrothed. My elder sister said that I should see the girl. I said, "Didi, where is the point in seeing the girl now? I should have seen her before betrothal." But she insisted. Word was sent to the girl's parents. They replied that three girls would pass by my house at 6 p.m. In the middle would be the betrothed girl in white saree and on her two sides would be her sister and sister-in-law in coloured sarees. I watched them from the window of my house. My betrothed did not look in my direction; so I could not see her face. But the white saree and her figure recalled the girl of the white launch that had been shown to me some years back. She was exactly that girl. I married her. I have had a very happy married life.

Many more examples can be cited which would fill a volume. Readers also would have had such experiences or known them from their relatives or friends. Conversation with God is not a rare phenomenon. It is a common experience of man. God is great—great in His mercy, great in His love.

18
Not a Leaf Moves Without His Will

If a person is in suffering or in pain or in trouble, he is often consoled by saying: You must accept all this as coming from God. Nothing happens except by His will. Not a leaf moves but by His will. This sets one thinking: If not a leaf moves without His will and there are hundreds of leaves on a tree, there are billions of trees in the world and there are trillions and trillions of leaves, so God shall have to use so many bits of His will to move all these innumerable leaves! If leaves move by His will, then other things must also be happening only by His will. Billions of waves on the surface of the water, clouds, rain drought, floods, wind, storms, cyclones, typhoons, earth-quakes, volcanic eruptions and other natural calamities also must be happening only by His will. All life—vegetable, bird, animal, human—must also be coming into existence by His will. Wars, fights, murders and all the human ills must be happening by His will. It seems God enjoys creating trouble in the world and is saddistic or whimsical. It does not sound well. Sages all the world over have described Him as all kind, all love. Then, is there something wrong with out thinking?

Leaves move only when the wind is blowing. If the wind is not blowing, the leaves do not move. So the cause of movement of the leaves is the wind. And why does the wind move? The wind moves because of the difference of temperature on the earth and its atmosphere. But where does the difference of temperature come from? It comes from the heat of the sun. And where does the heat of the sun come from? On the sun, there is gas burning and it is the burning of the gas that gives us light and heat. And who placed the gas there?

And so on. If you go on probing backwards, you will come to the first or the primordial cause. Thus, we find that the movement of the leaves is the effect, the cause of which is the movement of the wind; the movement of the wind is the effect, the cause of which is the difference in temperature; the difference in temperature is the effect, the cause of which is the heat of the sun; the heat of the sun is the effect, the cause of which is the burning of the gas and so forth. We see that everything has a cause and effect and nowhere does God come in.

When god decided to create, he created two principles—positive and negative; purusha and prakriti; soul and matter. These different names indicate the same thing. He then ordered prakriti to create. Prakriti created all things that exist in the whole creation. Then purusha permeated prakriti and the life began. Let us take human body. It is a dead body, it is a dead matter until the soul enters it, the soul permeates it. When the soul leaves the body, the body is a dead matter, it is matter, part of prakriti. This is also signified by the Shiva Linga Puja. Shiva Linga is the male or the positive principle penetrating the female or the negative principle and this is how life begins. Whenever there is an organisation or a Government, rules and regulations are framed for its smooth running. Prakriti also made laws for the smooth running of the creation. These are called the laws of nature, so that nature and Prakriti are made synonymous. Everything that is happening in the world, in this creation, happens according to the laws of nature. Nothing exists outside the laws of nature. The laws of a Government are made by its king. Laws of nature are made by God.

In a country when a person breaks a law, he is punished in accordance with the laws of the country and it is said that he was punished according to the law; it is not said that he was punished by the will of the king, though the laws were made by the king. Similarly, when a person is in suffering, that suffering is a punishment in accordance with the laws of nature. Why should it be said that his suffering is due to the will of God? To tell him that he must accept it as a will of God is to weaken his own will power and weaken his character. The proper thing is to tell him that his suffering is due to his violation of the laws of nature, that he must face it like a man and try to correct himself to mitigate the suffering. If he is told that, his will power is being strengthened, his character is being strengthened. He will try to correct himself and he should be told that if he puts forth effort, God will also help him because God helps those who help themselves.

It is said that by praying to one's God, suffering is lessened or altogether removed. If that be true, then where is the question of law. In a country, when a person is found guilty and punished and if he puts forth a prayer in a proper form to the king, the king may reduce his punishment or set aside the punishment. So also, if a prayer is put forth in a proper form to one's God, the God may relieve him of his suffering or set aside his suffering. God is above the law as the king is above the law; that is, they can take decision above the law.

Studying the life of those who have risen to the top of their profession, it is often found that a person has struggled hard against odds and impediments that came in his way and that he successfully got over them and reached the highest. Had he given up when he came across odds and impediments, accepting them as coming from God, he would never have risen. It is true that not everybody who has struggled hard has risen to the top or not everybody who has appealed to the king or God has got over his suffering or his suffering has been removed, but one should not forget that forgiveness from the king or God is not simply for the mere asking. It again depends upon various factors. To act is one's duty and it strengthens one's character. If the punishment is not removed immediately, one should feel that the effect of his cause, that is the punishment for his wrong-doing amounts to the same thing as his karma is paid out and that he has gone through the period of punishment. Understanding this will prevent the sufferer from lamenting, whining or whimpering. It will help him face his troubles with courage and determination and strengthen his character.

A few examples will make it clear how this understanding could be useful in every day life this will make life less painful and easier.

A friend of mine was suffering from indigestion. Anything he ate distressed him. Going the rounds of hospitals and doctors for twenty years brought him no relief. He was then advised to stop all medication, study the causes of indigestion and identify the causes of his trouble, whether it was indiscriminate eating, over-eating, wrong timings of eating, inadequate chewing, or whether any particular item of food caused him distress or any other factors. Accepting the advice, he undertook two years of dietary discipline along with some corresponding medication. He regained his normal digestion. He is now normal and happy. He can eat and digest everything. The cause of his suffering was breaking some digestive laws. Removing the error and obeying the laws of digestion, he got over the trouble. God did not come in the picture.

There was a renowned Pandit in Benaras. His name and fame had spread all over India. People from distant places went to him to get their difficulties solved. Once a man from Bombay went to see him and find out a solution to his difficulties. He knocked at the door of the Pandit's house. The door was opened by the Pandit's wife. On enquiring whether the Pandit was at home, the wife started abusing the Pandit, calling him names and said that she did know where the fellow was and banged the door shut in the face of the visitor. The visitor felt bewildered. He sat down on the steps outside his house to await his return. When the Pandit returned, he accousted the visitor cordially, took him inside the house and enquired the purpose of his visit. The visitor said that his affair could wait and he first wanted to understand the cause of the behaviour of his wife. The Pandit tried to evade the question but at the persistence of the visitor, he told him that in one of his past lives he was a crow and his present wife was a donkey. The donkey had a wound on its back. The crow would peck at the wound causing the donkey great pain who would run screaming. This went on day after day. One day the crow pecked at the wound so harsh that its beak got caught into the bone of the donkey and could not be freed. The donkey crying with pain ran headlong and fell into a river where both the donkey and crow got drowned. Now the crow was born as this Pandit and the donkey as his present wife. In the past, crow had pecked with his beak and now the wife was pecking with her tongue. The Pandit could have beaten his wife, turned her out or got rid of her to save himself from the suffering and the humiliation but he realised that his present suffering was the expiation of his past evil karma. If he postponed the payment by driving the wife out, he would have to pay later in future life. The karmic link would continue. But if he paid the price now, he would be free so, he accepted the situation willingly and lightly. In the suffering of the Pandit, there was no hand of God. The suffering was in the punishment of his evil karma.

I had to collect some medicine for my wife from the hospital. I was going on my cycle. I was keeping to the left of the road as required by the traffic rules. A bus was coming towards me from the front. As the bus neared me, a cyclist hit my cycle from the back. I lost my balance and I and my cycle fell to the right towards the road. By this time, the bus had reached the spot. The driver, seeing me falling, with great presence of mind, stopped the bus immediately. The commuters in the bus felt a great jolt and those standing in the bus fell forward. As the bus stopped, I fell on its mudguard and got a wound below my eye. A second's delay in stopping the bus would have found me crushed under its wheel. A friend in the bus recognised me, got down from it, came to me and picked me up and my cycle. He detained the cyclist and asked me what was to be done with him. I asked the cyclist how did he bang into me. He said that his cycle had no brakes. I reprimanded him for riding a cycle without brakes and asked my friend to let him go. The friend took me to a nearby hospital where the doctor dressed my wound and bandaged it. The friend offered to take me home. Instead I asked him to get me a tonga, put me and my cycle in it and accompany me. We went to the hospital, collected my wife's medicine and then he took me home. At home, I laughed and made light of the bandage because I did not want my wife to get perturbed. I could have thrashed the cyclist or called the police or confiscated his cycle, but I did nothing of the sort and let him go because I thought that the cyclist had not hurt me intentionally. We did not know each other. Therefore, this hurt must be the payment of some of my past evil karma against the cyclist and he had got his revenge. Had I got him into trouble, the whole karmic link would have continued. But by letting him go and accepting the punishment, I had freed myself from the karmic responsibility. Because of understanding of this law, my peace of mind was not disturbed. Considering that I was saved from the claws of death by an hair's breadth, I was not frightened, I was not nervous. I was not perturbed in any way and went about attending to my business in a normal way.

In order to got to college, I had to take two buses: the first one started from near my house. I had to get down – *route* to catch another bus which started from that place and would leave me at my college door. For the first bus, the ticket was five paise. Sometimes, the rush in the bus was so great that the conductor would not reach me by the time I had to get down to catch the other bus. I could not wait for the conductor to reach me because of the risk of my missing the second bus. Thus, this was a ticketless travel and I save five paise, though not deliberately or intentionally. In the evening, I used to return home from the college in a three-wheeler which cost me Rs. 1.05. But on the day when I was a ticketless commuter, the auto driver would ask me to pay Rs. 1.20. I would draw his attention to the meter which showed Rs. 1.05 but he would insist that I should pay Rs. 1.20, which I gladly did because I realised that enhanced payment was punishment for my ticketless travelling. I felt happy that my punishment was light and quick.

An old woman got erruptions on her whole body and there was unbearable itching and burning. She was restless and miserable. She sent word to her Guru praying that he has mercy on her and relieve her of her suffering. The Guru, in his reply, said that in her young age while snatching the gold necklace from a baby girl, she strangled her and threw her in a canal, not caring for the suffering she caused to her and to the parents who missed the baby. She had to pay for her evil deed, she should accept the suffering willingly and utter "Ram Nam" to lessen her suffering. The woman is since dead.

In everybody's life, there are several instances of suffering and pain. Each instance would require different treatment according to the conditions and the temperament of the sufferer. But the basic principles would be the same. Thus, understanding the basic principles will not only lighten one's suffering but also make one avoid taking wrong action and guide one to take right actions, leading one to righteousness.

19

Sikh Gurus

Some five hundred years ago, Guru Nanak appeared on the scene when Hindus were groaning under the persecution of the then rulers. Hindus were demoralised and almost ready to knuckle under. Guru Nanak came to the scene to help Hindus develop their self-respect, enhance their morals and make them have physical strength to face the tyranny. He realised that the task was too great to be completed in the life time of one individual. Hence, he developed the institution of 'Guruship', which went upto ten gurus. Upto the first five gurus, self-confidence and morale was attended to. From the sixth to the tenth guru, attention was paid to the physical or martial aspect as well, culminating in creating a militant section of the Hindus. This militant section was created by Guru Gobind Singh and was called 'Khalsas'.

The Gurudwaras built during the days of the gurus were built by Hindu Gurus with Hindu labour and Hindu money. Thus, they are Hindu Mandirs. Guru Granth Sahib contains sayings of the first five gurus and then the ninth guru, and they were all Hindus. The Granth was compiled by the fifth guru who was a Hindu. Granth Sahib therefore, is a scripture of the Hindus. In it, names of the Hindu Gods and their epithets occur thousands of times. Guru Nanak said that what he was saying was the original saying and he was only interpreting it. The truths that he has conveyed through his vanis' are the truths that were given to man by rishis, munis and sages of ancient India. He has conveyed them in the dialect of the time and suit the mental and emotional level of the people of the time. Thus, to call it a Sikh scripture is a misnomer. Similarly, to call these gurus as Sikh gurus, is not correct and to call them Hindu gurus is to labour the point. They are gurus of the Hindus, the Muslims, the Sikhs or any one who has belief in them and worships them. If Guru Gobind Singh had wanted the Sikh community to be a separate nation, he certainly would not have "ordered" (Hukam) the Sikhs to accept the Granth as their guru. To say anything different would be against the very purpose for which the gurus came and what they achieved.

Before creating the militant section, wanted blessings from a Hindu Devi. He performed the necessary *puja* with the help of a Brahman. The Devi appeared to him and blessed him and ordained that this militant section should have a hallmark of five 'kakas' - 'kangi', 'kes', 'kara', 'kirpan', and 'katcha', and that when Ardas was recited, it should begin with obeisance to the Devi (Bhagwati). Thus, Guru Gobind Singh never meant the new militant section to be a separate entity. It was a part of the Hindus, just as 'Kshatrias' are part of the four Hindu 'Varanas'.

The Muslims have more than one hundred sects. Principally, 'Sunis' and 'Shias' who keep on quarelling among themselves. But all of them call themselves Muslims and no sect has ever said that they are different from Muslims. Christianity also has many sects, but all of them call themselves Christians. In China, it is not uncommon that father, mother and son follow different religions and they have shrines in their home where they do their worship, but they do not quarrel among themselves or call themselves by the religion they profess. Everyone calls himself a 'Chinese'.

In India, this sense of separatism was created by the previous rulers. This was a device to divide and rule, and this wrong idea seems to have found a permanent place in our mind. We forget that we are Indians. This does not speak very high of our mental calibre. Unless, like the Chinese, we intensely feel that we are Indians - all of us - and consider religion as a personal affair and keep it out from politics, we will always be at loggerheads. No religion can prosper and be freely followed unless the nation is strong. The first consideration has to be that we are all one nation.

To combat the mischief of separatism, it will be wise on the past of Sikhs if they associate Hindus in running and administering the Gurudwaras and other religious institutions, as also while deserving the sacred religious days. One cannot forget the fact that not only are the Sikhs devotees of the ten gurus but also a very large number of Hindus.

20

Guru Nanak—A Unique Personality

Sri Krishna has said in the *Gita* that whenever ignorance and, therefore, sin increases in the world, He incarnates to guide man and lead him again to the path of righteousness.

Material forces ensnare man and lead him to indulge in sense-desires. When man becomes materialistic, he deviates from the path of righteousness, service and sacrifice. He becomes selfish and all the ills flowing therefrom invade his behaviour. He draws away from spiritual influences, and thus from his real self. God, then moved by His love for man, sends sages, messengers and prophets amidst men to remind them of their origin and of their essential spiritual nature and to reclaim them. They slip again and again, but God bears with them and time and again sends His emissaries to guide and uplift them. Every messenger gives some new dimension to the human development.

Guru Nanak was sent at such an hour. He came at a time when the religious zeal of the rulers to convert Hindus to their own religion placed Hinduism under a great stress. Hindus were placed under many handicaps and they were so much demoralised that they were almost ready to adopt the way of least resistance. Something was required to be done immediately to stem the onslaught of religious intolerance and persecution backed by temporal power. At such a time was this Master sent to restore self-confidence and self-respect among the people and develop in them the courage to defend and maintain their traditions and culture. The Hindu culture had reached its zenith thousands of years earlier, and for the past thousand years had been traversing the sloping curve. Continuous foreign invasions had accelerated the process of decay. Socially, economically and politically, the Hindus were sliding down. Rigid casteism, ignorance and superstition had invaded Hindu society. Higher castes disdained doing work that they thought was meant for the lower castes, with the result that they preferred to starve than work. Woman's position had deteriorated. Economically and politically, Hindus were at a great disadvantage. There was spiritual starvation.

As such a critical time, when things—temporal and spiritual—looked so dark, came Guru Nanak. He chose Punjab as His place of birth and as His field of work, because North India in general and the Sindhu-Punjab region in particular had suffered the most on account of a millenia of continuous raids and invasions by the foreign hordes through Sindh and Punjab.

The coming of Guru Nanak, followed by the other nine Gurus, was a unique experiment as also a unique incident in the spiritual history of the human race. There is no other example where a Master's work has been carried on by other Masters succeding Him. This was perhaps, because the work to be accomplished was not only a colossal one but the results, in order to be permanent, had to be consolidated through a few generations.

It was a Herculean task to raise the Hindus from the helplessness demoralisation and despondency in which they had fallen and to transform the cringing, hunted and down-trodden Hindus into a powerful, mighty and militant community of Sikhs, who, not only halted the inroads that the fanaticism of the rulers was making into Hinduism, but definitely broke the power of the alien ruler and succeeded in preserving the Hindu religion and the Hindu culture.

Guru Nanak's and the succeeding Gurus' teachings produced important reforms. Sikhism recognises no caste. All men are equal, irrespective of their calling and social positions. All sit together to eat in the community kitchen. Dignity of labour came to be recognised. Women found their place in society as equals.

All this produced far-roaching changes in the outlook of people. the Gurus also taught the path of spiritual development. The work was done systematically, stage by stage. In order to remove the old and replace it with the new, the teaching and the training was carried on for over one hundred years through the guruship of the ten gurus. And so was Guru Nanak succeeded by the nine Gurus to carry on and consolidate His mission.

It is always the down-trodden, lower strata of society - farmers, labourers, artisans and the like - that feels weaker because it is these people who have to bear the brunt of tyranny the most. Therefore, like the Christ, Guru Nanak started his work at the lower strata of society. This also helped give a new direction to the development of humanity, viz. the spirit of Brotherhood which, the occultists tell us, is the next main item of development of human culture. He chose a Muslim and a low class Hindu as His companions on His wanderings. This was a practical way of condemning the caste system. He had Hindus as also Muslims as His disciples. On His passing away, His body was claimed by both the communities and He transformed His mortal remains into roses which the two communities divided among themselves.

Guru Nanak found that the people were steeped in ignorance and superstition. Corruption was rampant. Knowledge, morality and all that is essential and sacred to human character was at its lowest level. Every one thought only of himself. Guru Nanak felt that the first step towards the uplift of people was to remove their ignorance and superstition and give them an ideal to work for. The second step was to create among them a sense of unity as without unity, nothing could be achieved. So, through music and verse, through His conduct and through His extensive preaching tours, He tried to dispel ignorance and superstition. He disclaimed all gods and goddesses. He taught that all religions were only different expositions of the same one reality; that there was only one God, the Father of all humanity; that all human beings were children of the same one God and, therefore, equal; that castes and social divisions were unjust. He thus set out to create a society that believed in Brotherhood. He, thus, succeeded in uniting people together as one family to work for its own upliftment and progress. In order to build the individual and national character. He taught the practice of purity, patience, fearing the wrong, cultivating love for fellow-beings and uttering the Divine Name (Nam). He also showed the uselessness of the ceremonials. In order that what He preached may go direct to the heart, He gave His teaching in the dialect prevailing at the time. To give practical shape to His teachings, He enjoined on His followers to open schools; to have 'satsang' and congregational singing and to partake food in the community kitchen (langar). Thus, He developed in His people a sense of self-respect and national sentiment and set before them an Ideal to work for.

21
Mind and Body

All thoughts, of whatever nature they be, leave their impress on the brain and through the brain on the body. The science of Physiognomy is based on this reaction of the thought of the body. Everyone gets good, bad or indifferent thoughts. The final outcome of one's thoughts determines whether one is good or bad. If good in him outbalances evil, the person is good and vice versa. The impress produced on the brain is not lost; it remains there as a seed. It grows and sprouts and prompts thinking of similar thoughts again. Thoughts lead to action. According to the yogic philosophy, the germs of thoughts - or impulses or instincts - remain in the *Muladhara* (the lower end of the spinal column). This region is supposed to be the storehouse of the impulses, imbibed through lives and are carried from one incarnation to another. They can be destroyed only when one gets a glimpse of the Divine or when one reaches Nirvikalpa Samadhi - the stage when he gives up all attachments. This action and reaction of the body and the mind in their turn, re-act on the mind of the human race as a whole, and bodies of the individuals composing the race.

It is well known that one is easily affected by atmosphere. If one is in a temple, one feels devotional; if in a hilarious company, the mood becomes hilarious. In the company of irritable people, one feels irritable and so on. The effect of the atmosphere is all the more pronounced if one is already prone to that attitude of mind. For example, devotional temperament gets more strongly affected in a temple than a non-devotional temperament. A light-hearted individual is more easily carried away in a hilarious company than a grave person.

Thus an individual not only affects himself but the whole human race, for better or for worse.

Since every thought leaves its impress on the brain, and so on the whole life and the cycle of lives, it affords a method of improving oneself and combating evil. For example, when one is irritable and short-tempered and one decided that he shall not be irritated; he shall not be upset; he shall remain balanced in the face of any provocation, this thought itself will produce its fruit and combat the previous irritability, albeit it will take time and perservance and in proportion to the force of the irritability. It has been done and can be done.

SELF-DISCIPLINE

Everyone has one or the other fault. Faults give rise to improper behaviour. Improper behaviour hurts others. They observe it and criticise it and sometimes try to correct the person. This correction is more often than not resented.

Does this correction help? The fault is within me. How can anyone show me what is within me? I alone can see it. Anyone else's effort to show me will only obstruct me from seeing it. Others can only see my conduct, but they cannot see and realise the cause that gives rise to my behaviour. I alone can see it and should be left alone to see it. And if and when I see it, I can correct it - I alone can correct it.

SUFFERING

There is so much suffering in life. Particularly at the present time, we feel it acutely. It has drawn our attention more poignantly.

But suffering there has always been, ever since life began. An individual, a community, a nation - they are all continously passing through suffering. An individual is born with a cry and dies with a gasp, and in between all his life, he struggles. History tells us how communities have had to wander from place to place either because of want of food or other encounters or because a more powerful community drove them off. A nation goes to war against another, causing terrible carnage and suffering. All this has existed since time immemorial. It looks as if suffering is a part of life. Wherever there is life, there is suffering. It is as universal as air or sunshine. Yet it is difficult to believe that God who created life also created pain and suffering.

What then is suffering? What is it due to? What is its origin and its purpose? What is its necessity and place in life? How can we get over it? If we understand it, we shall have understood suffering. And to understand it is to conquer it.

Suffering is necessary to get into the mood of searching truth. A river takes its course and always runs along the same path, not caring whether the path it has taken is useful or not, whether it is helpful to the living being or not. If the path is useful, nobody bothers about it but if it is not, man tries to divert it along a more useful channel by putting a dam or an obstacle in its way. If the obstacle is too great for the river to cross over, it diverts its path and takes another course. If, it has taken a course which is now useful, it serves its purpose and is nearer the truth.

Suffering may, therefore, be taken as due to obstruction. In the case of a human being, obstruction to what? Obstruction to his 'I-hood'. I hood is ignorance. It eclipses the reality and keeps one away from the truth. God, nature or the power that guides evolution desires that we all perceive the truth. But truth can be perceived only by removing the self.

One has always to be on the alert. Life is a continuous struggle between the opposing forces; forces that try to drown us, forces that want to draw us into the vortex. It is a struggle between the positive and the negative forces or the forces of darkness and light, and one cannot afford to be slack.